A Practical Guide to
RUSSIAN STRESS

A Practical Guide to
RUSSIAN STRESS

JAMES FORSYTH

LECTURER IN RUSSIAN
UNIVERSITY OF GLASGOW

OLIVER & BOYD
EDINBURGH AND LONDON

OLIVER AND BOYD LTD.

Tweeddale Court
Edinburgh 1

39a Welbeck Street
London W.1

First published 1963

Printed in Great Britain
by Robert Cunningham and Sons Ltd, Alva

PREFACE

This book is intended as a practical guide to Russian stress (and to some extent a reference book) for those who, in learning to speak Russian, have reached a stage where they feel some sort of systematic attack on this problem is necessary. It must be admitted that no set of rules of stress can be devised which is both completely exhaustive and simple. Nevertheless, words with similar stress patterns can be grouped together to give a number of more or less comprehensive rules as well as some general pointers which are fairly reliable for practical purposes. Categorical rules in Russian always court suspicion, and the author's excuse for an occasional rough-and-ready approximate rule is that exceptions and exceptions to exceptions can always be found. As it is, quite a large number of exeeptions will be found here, where the authorities on the subject show more than one 'permissible' pattern – a matter on which various Russian authorities sometimes disagree.

The learner is naturally more troubled by words which have mobile stress than by those with fixed stress, and by smaller groups with marked idiosyncrasies rather than by large uncomplicated groups. Consequently relatively few examples have been given under the more general and categorical rules which cover large numbers of common words (cf. the notes to the Index on p. 123). On the other hand, the more particular the rule and the smaller the number of words it covers, the more exhaustive is the list of examples, sometimes including relatively uncommon words.

The book consists of two parts. The main purpose of Part I is to give rules determining whether a word has fixed or mobile stress, and patterns of mobile stress with lists of examples. Word-formation and the position of the accent in basic forms (nominative singular of nouns and adjectives, infinitives of verbs) cannot be entirely divorced from this however, and in Part I suffixes are listed which are either always stressed or always unstressed. Part II deals with Word-formation alone, particularly those suffixes which may be stressed or unstressed, and with certain special classes of words—diminutives, proper names, etc.

The words covered in this book are as far as possible restricted to those which are not only useful but essential to anyone learning to speak Russian, and it is based on a fairly restricted vocabulary as a starting point (compiled largely on the basis of *The Russian Word Count* by H. H. Josselson, Detroit, 1953). As the aim is neither an exhaustive academic classification nor a statistical survey the author has tried to resist the collection of non-essential curiosities. For words beyond the scope of this book the essential reference book is Русское литературное произношение и ударение: словарь-справочник by R. I. Avanesov and S. I. Ozhegov. This work has usually been my authority in qualifying various forms as 'normal', 'permissible', 'archaic', etc.

I am indebted to Professor Kenneth Brooke for his encouragement to undertake such a book, to Mr Peter Henry for advice and criticism at all stages, to Mr Dennis Ward for valuable comments on the manuscript, and to my wife for assistance in reading the proofs.

J.F.

CONTENTS

PART I

STRESS IN BASIC PARTS OF SPEECH

Normal abbreviations for the cases are used throughout.

With nouns, where a form is given in brackets without description it is the genitive singular.

Verbs are Imperfective unless marked (pfv.). Consonant changes in the present tense of verbs (first person singular) are indicated in brackets, e.g. **ходи́ть** (**д/ж**), i.e. present is **хожу́, хо́дит**, etc.

All cross-references are to sections (§) not pages.

The phonetic transcriptions used in a few places to illustrate pronunciation employ the International Phonetic Association alphabet as it is applied to Russian in Boyanus' *Russian Pronunciation*, London, 1955.

PART I

STRESS IN BASIC PARTS OF SPEECH

CHAPTER 1

GENERAL

§1. In Russian, accentuation is so intimately bound up with other factors determining pronunciation that, although we cannot attempt to deal here with the total role of stress in pronunciation, we must briefly recall the main points.

(*a*) Stressed syllables are produced with more force of breath (and are somewhat louder and longer) than unstressed syllables, which tend to be reduced and weakened to a greater or less degree. There is a characteristic pattern according to which the varying degrees of stress are distributed. Within a polysyllabic word like **фотогра́фия** *photography*, the syllable pronounced with greatest force is **-граф-**; the syllable immediately preceding this stressed syllable, **-то-**, has the next, intermediate degree of stress, and the other syllables have the weakest stress. (In them the stress is not entirely equal, final syllables being weakest of all.) The distribution of stress in a long word can therefore be represented graphically in this way:

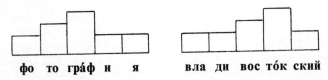

This contrasts with the characteristic pattern of stress in English, in which the syllable immediately preceding the stressed syllable is one of the weakest, the second degree of stress being given to the second syllable before the stress, e.g.

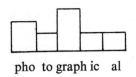

The assimilation of the Russian pattern of stress distribution is essential for correct pronunciation, since unstressed vowels are reduced to a greater or less degree according to their position.

(*b*) Unstressed **o** is pronounced as follows: in the syllable immediately preceding the stressed syllable – [a], e.g. **вода́** [vaˡda]; in any other syllable preceding or following the stressed syllable as a neutral vowel [ə] (similar to the sound of **a** in the English words *sofa, about*). e.g. **водопровод** [vədəpra¹vɔt] *water-pipe*; **доктор** [¹dɔktər]; **слово** [¹slɔvə]. But at the beginning of a word, not preceded by a consonant, it is pronounced [a], e.g. **оборот** [aba¹rɔt] *a turn, revolution*. In connected speech such an initial unstressed **o** is reduced to [ə], e.g. **от одного** [atədna¹vɔ].

(*c*) Unstressed **a** has exactly the same sounds in corresponding positions as unstressed **o**, e.g. **Казахстан** [kəzax¹stan] *Kazakhstan*; **делала** [dɛlələ]; but initially **ананас** [ana¹nas] *pineapple*.

(*d*) Unstressed **e** is pronounced as a narrow vowel similar to that in the word *pig* – [ɪ], e.g. **перевод** [pɪrɪ¹vɔt] *translation*.

(*e*) It is because the pronunciation of a vowel changes according to its position with reference to the accented syllable that the assimilation of correct stress patterns is important. Both the correct pronunciation and the correct interpretation of a given form depend on stress, for example in the various forms of the word **сторона** *side*, with accusative **сторону** and genitive plural **сторон** [stəra¹na; ¹stɔrənu; sta¹rɔn], or of **ходить** *to go*, with **я хожу, он ходит** [xa¹dɪt̪; jaxa¹ʒu; ɔn¹xɔdɪt], which differ widely in their phonetic make-up. If one does not know these patterns the whole 'shape' of a word with mobile stress seems fluid and unreliable.

(*f*) The pronunciation of a given morpheme* varies also according to the accentuation of various words derived from the parent word, giving such results as the various pronunciations of the basic 'word' **город** in: **город** *town*, **огород** *kitchen-garden*, **городок** *little town*, **пригород** *suburb*, pronounced [¹gɔrət, aga¹rɔt, gəra¹dɔk, ¹prigərət]. Word-building as such is dealt with in Chapters 9-12.

§2. The tendency for **e** and **ё** to interchange is of course bound up with stress: remember that in any word containing **ё** the syllable containing it is the accented syllable, and that often when the accent moves on to **e** its pronunciation changes to **ё**, e.g. **село** *village*, with pl. **сёла**; and conversely that a **ё** syllable losing its stress reverts to **e**, e.g. **нёс, несла**.

§3. The spelling can indicate the position of the accent in words where the sibilants **ж, ш, щ** and the affricates **ц, ч** are followed by a syllable containing the vowel **o** or **e**, e.g. **мешок** *bag* is bound to have

---

* *Morpheme*: a minimum meaningful element of a word – root, prefix, suffix, etc., as distinct from a syllable, which is simply a phonetic 'chunk' of a word, usually defined by position. For instance in the English verb 'condúct' and noun 'condúctor' the accent falls on the same morpheme -*duct*-, which is the last syllable in the former but the penultimate in the latter. In the noun 'cónduct', however, the accent is on the penultimate syllable, but on a different morpheme *con*-.

the accent on the suffix: **мешо́к**; while **ча́шек** *cups* (gen.pl.) is bound
to have the accent on the stem: **ча́шек**. The reason for this is that
after these consonants **о** not **ё** is written in a stressed position, and **e**
in an unstressed position in noun and adjective suffixes and endings.
Other examples are:

ножо́м *knife* (instr.)	**му́жем** *husband* (instr.)
свечо́й *candle* (instr.)	**ту́чей** *cloud* (instr.)
старичо́к *old man* (dimin.)	**цвето́чек** *flower* (dimin.)
большо́го *big* (gen.sing.)	**хоро́шего** *good* (gen.sing.)
лицо́ *face*	**со́лнце** *sun*
отцо́м *father* (instr.)	**кита́йцем** *Chinese* (instr.)
плащо́м *raincoat* (instr.)	**о́бщем** *general* (prep.sing.masc.)

This applies to the writing of all noun and adjective suffixes and
case endings (except the foreign suffix **-ёр** from French *-eur*, e.g.
дирижёр (*orchestra*) *conductor*, cf. **режиссёр** *producer* (*of a play,
film*)).

But in verb endings, **e** is written after these consonants even if the
syllable is stressed (**ё**), e.g.

плачет (**пла́чет**) *weeps*	**печет** (**печёт**) *bakes*
ношенный (**но́ш-**) *carried*	**решенный** (**решённый**) *decided*

Within the stems or roots of words of all categories **e** (**ё**) is however
usually written after these consonants even when stressed (usually in
these words mobile stress in some forms leaves the stem unstressed),
e.g.

желтый (**жёлтый**) *yellow* – fem. short form: **желта́**
шелк (**шёлк** *silk*) – pl. **шелка́**
черт (**чёрт, чорт**) *the devil* – gen.pl. **черт́ей**

In unstressed syllables after **ж, ч, ш, щ** and **ц**, however, **о** is never
written in the stem of Russian words, but may appear in foreign
words, e.g. **жоке́й** *jockey*, **шокола́д** *chocolate*.

Proper names sometimes retain archaic spellings which do not conform to these rules – cf. § 135*a*.

§4. Sometimes the position of stress differentiates between a pair of
otherwise homonymous words, e.g.

за́мок	*castle*	**замо́к**	*lock*
хло́пок	*cotton*	**хлопо́к**	*clap of the hands*
му́ка	*torment*	**мука́**	*flour*
а́тлас	*atlas*	**атла́с**	*satin*
у́же	*narrower*	**уже́**	*already*
па́рить	*to steam*	**пари́ть**	*to soar*

          Ма́шина маши́на   *Masha's car*

Cf. §§28, 46, 55, 56, 74, 80, 20*a*, 135*c-d*.

§5. In other pairs there is a stylistic difference; for example, as well as the normal forms **молодéц** *fine fellow, well done!* **дéвица** *spinster*, one finds in folklore **дóбрый мóлодец, крáсна дéвица** *fair maiden*; beside **мéньший** *smaller, lesser* there is the colloquial **меньшóй брат** *younger brother.*

§6. In some words alternative stress patterns exist, both being equally 'permissible', e.g. **инáче** or **и́наче** *otherwise.* Cf. §§12, 38, 39, 135.

§7. In general any given Russian word of two or more syllables has only one stressed syllable, e.g. **Владивостóк**; but some long compound words, in which the two or more components to some extent retain their individuality, have one (or more) secondary stress, which is always the earlier of two stresses. This is marked here by a grave accent `, e.g. **машѝностроéние** *mechanical engineering*, **желѐзобетóн** *reinforced concrete*, **элѐктропромы́шленность** *electrical industry*, **свѐтлокрáсный** *light red*, **тёмнокрáсный** *dark red*, **церкòвнославя́нский** *Church Slavonic*, **дèревообрабáтывающий** *woodworking.* Similarly some shorter compounds, e.g. **кѝнофи́льм** *film.*

Compound abbreviations particularly tend to have secondary stress, even in short words, e.g. **сòцстрáх** *social insurance*, **дрàмкружóк**, *drama club.*

On the other hand, there are very long compound words of frequent occurrence which have no secondary stress, e.g. **железнодорóжный** *railway*, **сельскохозя́йственный** *agricultural*, **восьмидесятилéтний** *octogenarian.*

There are several prefixes which usually bear a secondary stress, e.g. **пòслевоéнный** *post-war*, **свèрхъестéственный** *supernatural*, **кòнтрреволю́ция** *counter-revolution*, **àнтирелигиóзный** *anti-religious*, **прòсовéтский** *pro-Soviet.* (But *not*, of course, the Russian prefix in e.g. **проходи́ть.**) Also the prefixes **àрхи-, сỳпер-, трàнс-, у́льтра-.**

§8. The chief difficulty of Russian accentuation, however, is not the stress of words in their basic forms (nominative singular of nouns and adjectives, infinitive of verbs), words at rest as it were, but the way in which the accent moves from one syllable to another within a given word in the various grammatical forms in which it occurs in speech. While the main emphasis in the first part of this book is on the latter aspect, the position of accent in basic forms has also been dealt with to some extent, particularly in Pt. II.

§9. The forms which present difficulties of accentuation are nouns, predicative (short form and comparative) adjectives, and various parts of the verb (present tense, past tense, and past participle passive). General guiding principles on accentuation applicable to several parts of speech are very few, namely:

(*a*) Nouns and verbs of three or more syllables in the basic form tend to have the stress fixed on the same syllable of the basic form (strictly: the same morpheme) throughout all other forms, e.g. челове́к, организа́ция, бога́тый, полити́ческий, рабо́тать, благодари́ть.

(*b*) Words with the accent falling not on the ending but on an earlier syllable of the basic form, tend to have fixed stress. (This cannot be said of adjectives), e.g. това́рищ, же́нщина, кни́га, прави́тельство, де́лать, гото́вить.

(*c*) Nouns and verbs with the accent falling on the ending in the basic form very often have mobile accent, e.g. рука́, борода́, окно́, получи́ть.

(*d*) Common monosyllabic (and many disyllabic) words very often have mobile stress, e.g. стол *table*, жена́ *wife*, сло́во *word*, нов, нова́ etc. *new*, мочь *to be able*.

But these 'rules' are too vague to be useful, and in the following chapters the various parts of speech will be dealt with separately.

Chapter 2

NOUNS

NOMINATIVE SINGULAR. (This section, §§ 10-12, is not concerned with the question whether the accent in the paradigm of a given word is mobile or fixed.)

§ 10. General rules for the position of stress in the nominative singular of nouns are few, and apply only to derived nouns with suffixes. The most useful are the following (other suffixes are dealt with in §§ 113-132):

(*a*) The following suffixes always bear the accent in the nom. sg.:

-ак/-як	дура́к *fool*, рыба́к *fisherman*
-ёнок (and pl. **-я́та**)	ребёнок *child*, котёнок *kitten*
-о́нок (and pl. **-а́та**)	волчо́нок *wolf cub*
-ёж/-еж	платёж *payment*, рубе́ж *boundary*
-аж (French *-age*)	шпиона́ж *espionage*, камуфля́ж *camouflage*
-ист	коммуни́ст *Communist*, эгои́ст *egoist* (cf. § 127)
-изм	социали́зм *Socialism*, куби́зм *Cubism* (cf. § 127)
-о́нка/-ёнка	собачо́нка *little dog*, сестрёнка *sister* (cf. § 129*d*)
-а́тор	дикта́тор *dictator*, коммента́тор *commentator*
-у́ра	литерату́ра *literature*, диктату́ра *dictatorship* (there are a few exceptions, e.g. конура́ *kennel*, where **-ура** is not in fact a suffix)

(*b*) The following suffixes are always unstressed:

-ик	*as a diminutive suffix only*: e.g. сто́лик *little table*, до́мик *little house* (see also § 114)
-чик	лётчик *airman*, шка́фчик *little cupboard* (otherwise **-ик, -щик** and **-ник** are sometimes stressed, sometimes not, e.g. учени́к *pupil*, рабо́тник *workman*: cf. § 114)
-тель	учи́тель *teacher*, дви́гатель *engine* (cf. § 125). (There are a few exceptions in which **-тель** is in fact not an added suffix, e.g. оте́ль (*m.*) *hotel*, кани́тель (*f.*) *long-drawn-out proceedings*.)

red tape

-ка	де́вочка *girl*, кни́жка *book(let)* (even when the original noun has stress on the ending, e.g. рука́—ру́чка; вода́ – во́дка; борода́ – боро́дка: see also §§116*a*, 117, 129*a*)
-онька/-енька	ма́менька *Mummy* (cf. §129*a*)
-ша	конду́кторша *conductress*, миллионе́рша *millionairess* (cf. §116)
-ость	ра́дость *joy*, промы́шленность *industry* (cf. §121)
-ышко	(even when the original noun has stress on the ending) e.g. гнездо́ *nest* – гнёздышко *little nest*

(*c*) **-ец**. Most words of three syllables ending in **-ец**, and all of more than three, have the **-ец** unstressed, the accent usually falling on the syllable before the suffix, e.g. кита́ец *a Chinese*, иностра́нец *foreigner*, whereas most words of two syllables have the accent on **-ец** (and therefore mobile stress: see below §19*b*), e.g. оте́ц *father*, купе́ц *merchant*, коне́ц *end*. This suffix is dealt with in more detail in §115.

(*d*) **-анин**. Most nouns with this suffix have stress as in англича́нин *Englishman*, крестья́нин *peasant*, and fixed throughout on the same syllable (plurals: англича́не, крестья́не). Similarly nouns of class or nationality in **-ин**, e.g. ба́рин *lord, nobleman* (pl. ба́ре), тата́рин *Tartar* (pl. тата́ры). Some, however, have stress on the last syllable in the nominative singular, and moving back one or more syllables in the plural (all cases), e.g. христиани́н *a Christian* – pl. христиа́не, христиа́н, христиа́нам. Similarly мещани́н *a townsman of the lower class*, славяни́н *a Slav*, дворяни́н *a nobleman*, армяни́н *an Armenian*. Граждани́н *citizen*, has stress on the first syllable in the plural: гра́ждане, гра́ждан, гра́жданам.

(*e*) **-ор**. This suffix is nearly always unstressed (and **-а́тор** and **-и́тор** always have the accent on **а** and **и**), e.g. конду́ктор *conductor*, консерва́тор *Conservative*, телеви́зор *television set*, компози́тор *composer*. Exceptions are коридо́р *corridor*, and мото́р *motor*.

(*f*) **-лог**. Words ending in this syllable are either connected with the verb **-ложить**, in which case they have the accent on **-лог**, e.g. зало́г *pledge*, нало́г *tax*, предло́г *pretext, preposition*; or derived from Greek *logos*, in which case the accent is usually on the syllable preceding **-лог**, e.g. антропо́лог *anthropologist*, био́лог *biologist*, гео́лог *geologist*. Exceptions with stress on the last syllable include катало́г *catalogue*, проло́г *prologue*, эпило́г *epilogue*. (Compare stress in some other words derived from Greek, e.g. ана́том *anatomist*, диа́гноз *diagnosis*, иеро́глиф *hieroglyph*, сино́ним *synonym*, etc.)

(*g*) **-ота**. This suffix is usually stressed, e.g. **красота́** *beauty*, **высота́** *height*; but there are some exceptions with stress on the second last syllable, e.g. **дремо́та** *drowsiness*, **охо́та** *hunting*, **рабо́та** *work*; or on the stem in **гра́мота** *reading and writing, charter* (cf. § 22*a*). (In some of these exceptions **-ота** is in fact not a suffix.)

(*h*) **-ия**. This suffix is generally unstressed in nearly all common words, e.g. **ли́ния** *line*, **на́ция** *nation*, **администра́ция** *administration*. But in some technical terms in literature, history, philosophy and science, and many medical terms, stress is on the **и**, e.g. **стихи́я** *element*, **литурги́я** *liturgy*, **тирани́я** *tyranny*, **симметри́я** *symmetry*, **хирурги́я** *surgery*, **терапи́я** *therapy*. Note the stress of the noun *bourgeoisie* **буржуази́я** (stress on **-аз-** is considered old-fashioned). *Metallurgy* may be stressed either **металлурги́я** or **металлу́ргия**. Note the difference in stress between **Росси́я** *Russia* and **Малоросси́я** *Little Russia, Ukraine* and **Белору́ссия** *White Russia*.

(*j*) **-ие** and **-ье**. These suffixes are generally unstressed, e.g. **усло́вие** *condition*, **ле́звие** *blade*, **разви́тие** *development*, **собы́тие** *event*, **сча́стье** *happiness*.

But in a few words these endings are stressed, e.g. **бельё** *linen, underclothing*, **ружьё** *gun*, **бытьё** *life*, **бытие́** *being, existence*, **житие́** *life* (*of a saint*).

The suffix **-ние** is always unstressed, e.g. **мне́ние** *opinion*, **основа́ние** *foundation*. See further §125.

(*k*) **-ство**. This suffix is unstressed except in a few words, e.g. **чу́вство** *feeling*, **прави́тельство** *government*, **госуда́рство** *state*, **иску́сство** *art*; but **вещество́** *substance, matter*, **существо́** *being, creature*, **большинство́** *majority* (cf. §§18, 122).

§11. The prefix вы-. Stress of nouns with this prefix derived from verbs depends on the nature of the derivative suffix used rather than the aspect of the verb from which the noun is derived (cf. § 68), e.g. **выходи́ть** *to go/come out* is imperfective, but the noun is **вы́ход** *exit;* and on the other hand **вы́ступить** *to step forward, perform* is perfective, but the noun is **выступле́ние** *performance*.

The accent is on the prefix **вы-** in:

(*a*) Suffixless masculine nouns (chiefly disyllabic), e.g. **вы́бор** *choice*, **вы́воз** *export*, **вы́говор** *reproof*, **вы́езд** *departure*.

(*b*) Feminine nouns with the suffix **-а** or **-ка**, e.g. **вы́года** *advantage*, **вы́дача** *giving out, distribution*, **вы́веска** *shop-sign*, **вы́ставка** *exhibition*.

The accent is not on the prefix **вы-** in:

(*a*) Nouns with the suffix **-ание, -ение**, e.g. **выпи́сывание** *writing out*, **вычита́ние** *subtraction*, **вычисле́ние** *calculation*, **выполне́ние** *fulfilment*.

(*b*) Nouns with the suffix **-тель**, e.g. **выключа́тель** *electric switch*, **вытрезви́тель** '*cooler*' *for drunks*.

Adjectives derived from such nouns do not necessarily retain the same stress as the noun, e.g. **вы́ход** *exit* has **выходно́й**; **вы́воз** *export* has **вывозно́й** (cf. §147).

§12. The position of the accent in the nominative singular varies in a few nouns, e.g. **библиоте́ка** *library* is the accepted pronunciation, whereas formerly a common pronunciation was **библио́тека**. Similarly **при́нцип** *principle* was formerly **принци́п**. *Tvorog*, a kind of sweet cream cheese, can be pronounced either **творо́г** or **тво́рог**.

§13. The accent is fixed on the same syllable throughout all forms in a very large proportion of the total number of Russian nouns; but in a very high proportion of common, everyday nouns it is mobile.

§14. Most common short masculine nouns have mobile stress (cf. §§19, 20, 21, 24*c*; and exceptions in §16*d*).

§15. All feminine and neuter nouns with accent on the ending in the nominative singular have mobile stress (with a few exceptions, cf. §16*b*).

NOUNS WITH FIXED STRESS

§16. Nouns with fixed stress fall into the following categories:

(*a*) **Most nouns of three or more syllables in the nom.sg. have fixed accent throughout.** (Exceptions, especially masculine nouns with stressed suffixes, feminine nouns with stress on the ending, and a few neuters, are listed below in §§ 19*b*, 20*a*, 20*b*, 22*a*, 22*b*, 24, 25.) Only a few examples of these very large groups of nouns with fixed stress are given here:

(i) Masculine

авто́бус	*bus*	**рабо́тник**	*workman*
англича́нин	*Englishman*	**телефо́н**	*telephone*
крестья́нин	*peasant*	**това́рищ**	*comrade*
материа́л	*material*	**университе́т**	*university*
мужчи́на	*man*	**челове́к**	*human being*
парохо́д	*steamship*	**ю́ноша**	*youth*

For the stress of **граждани́н** *citizen* and other similar nouns see §10*d*.

(ii) Feminine: **All feminine nouns of three or more syllables with non-final stress in the nom.sg. have fixed stress throughout.** (In fact an even more comprehensive rule occurs under §16*b* below.)

де́вушка	*girl*	не́нависть	*hatred*
доро́га	*road*	полови́на	*half*
ко́мната	*room*	промы́шленность	*industry*
ле́топись	*chronicle*	соба́ка	*dog*
неде́ля	*week*	у́лица	*street*

An isolated exception to this is дере́вня (see §21*b*).

(iii) Neuter:

боло́то	*marsh*	здоро́вье	*health*
воро́та (pl.)	*gate*	учрежде́ние	*establishment*
пра́вило	*rule*	о́бщество	*society*
я́блоко (pl. я́блоки) *apple*		прави́тельство	*government*

Exceptions are зе́ркало, о́блако, о́зеро, де́рево (all in §20*b* below) and колесо́, ремесло́ etc. (in §22*b* below), which have mobile stress.

(*b*) The following feminine and neuter nouns with only two syllables in the nom.sg. have fixed stress:

(i) Feminine: **All feminine nouns of the -a declension with stress not on the ending in the nom.sg. have fixed stress throughout** (including nouns of three or more syllables). Only a few examples of these very numerous nouns are given:

ве́ра	*belief*	ры́ба	*fish*
кни́га	*book*	си́ла	*strength*
пе́сня (g.pl. пе́сен) *song*		ту́ча	*cloud*
пти́ца	*bird*	шко́ла	*school*

Despite §15 above, a number of feminine nouns with the accent falling on the ending in the nom.sg. have it fixed throughout on the endings, e.g.

госпожа́	*Mrs, lady*	похвала́	*praise*
еда́	*food, meal*	раба́	*slave*
жара́	*heat (of weather)*	скамья́ (g.pl.	
зола́	*ashes*	скаме́й)	*bench*
икра́	*caviare*	статья́ (g.pl.	
клевета́	*slander*	стате́й)	*article*
княжна́ (g.pl.	*princess*	струя́ (g.pl.	
княжо́н)		струй)	*jet, stream*
конура́ (g.pl.	*kennel*	тайга́	*taiga*
кону́р)		тоска́	*melancholy*
кочерга́	*poker*	черта́	*feature*
мечта́ (no g.pl.) *dream*			

(ii) Feminine **-ь** declension: only some of these nouns have fixed stress (but they include all those of three or more syllables, with a few exceptions). Common examples are:

боль	*pain*	ткань	*cloth*
грязь†	*dirt*	цель	*aim*
даль†	*distance*	честь†	*honour*
ель	*fir*	болéзнь	*illness*
жизнь	*life*	кровáть	*bed(stead)*
кровь†	*blood*	óсень	*autumn*
мель†	*sandbank*	пáмять	*memory*
мысль	*thought*	печáть	*seal, press*
пыль†	*dust*	пóмощь	*help*
связь†	*bond, con-*	постéль	*bed(ding)*
	nection	тетрáдь	*notebook*

† These have the ending stressed in the locative singular only, e.g. **о пы́ли** but **в пыли́; в связи́ с** *in connection with.*

For feminine nouns of this declension with mobile stress, see §§21*b*, 19*d*.

(iii) Neuter: A limited number of basic disyllabic neuter nouns have fixed stress, e.g.

блю́до	*dish*	крéсло	*armchair*
вéко (pl. вéки)	*eyelid*	плáтье	*dress*
гóре	*grief*	сóлнце	*sun*
гóрло	*throat*	у́тро*	*morning*

*Note, however, fixed phrases with **утро**, with stress on the endings: **до утрá, от утрá, с утрá, к утру́, по утрáм; шесть часóв утрá** 6 *a.m.*, but **красотá у́тра** *the beauty of the morning.*

(Generally the stress of disyllabic neuter nouns alternates in singular and plural: see §20*b*, 22*b*.)

(*c*) **Feminine and neuter derived nouns with suffixes, and abstract nouns in general,** have fixed stress.

(i) Feminine: particularly those with suffixes **-ость** and **-ия**. Only a few examples of various types are given:

рáдость	*joy*	тишинá (no pl.)	*silence*
возмóжность	*possibility*	ширинá (no pl.)	*width*
дрýжба (no pl.)	*friendship*	лúния	*line*
борьбá (no pl.)	*struggle*	истóрия	*history*

But note that nouns with suffixes **-отá, -инá**, which have plural forms, e.g. **красотá** *beauty*, **глубинá** *depth*, have mobile stress (see §22a), as have **любо́вь** *love* (see §17c), **ско́рость** *speed* and a few other nouns ending in **-ость** (see §21b).

(ii)   Neuter: particularly those with suffixes **-ство** and **-ие**. Only a few examples with various suffixes are given:

сча́стье	*happiness*	чу́вство	*feeling*
развти́ие	*development*	о́бщество	*society*
зна́ние	*knowledge*	существо́	*being*
возвраще́ние	*return*	учи́лище	*school*

Nouns with stressed ending **-ьё** may have mobile accent, e.g. **ружьё** (cf. §22b).

(d)   Masculine nouns with fixed stress.

(i)   Only a limited number of monosyllabic masculine nouns have fixed stress, e.g.

бег†	*running*	рост	*growth, stature*
брак	*marriage*	свет	*light*
брат (pl. бра́тья,		слух	*hearing*
бра́тьев)	*brother*	смех	*laughter*
бред†	*delirium*	смысл	*sense*
быт†	*day-to-day life*	спор	*argument*
взгляд	*glance*	срок	*fixed time*
вид†	*view, aspect, etc.*	стиль	*style*
внук	*grandson*	страх	*fear*
гнев	*anger*	строй	*system, order* (cf. §20a)
дед	*grandfather*	стул (pl. сту́лья,	
дух	*spirit*	сту́льев)	*chair*
жар	*heat*	фунт	*pound*
звук	*sound*	храм	*temple*
знак	*sign*	цех(†)	*workshop*
крик	*cry*	член	*member*
мак	*poppy*	шум	*noise*
нрав	*disposition*	юг	*south*
пот†	*sweat*	яд	*poison*
рак	*crayfish*		

†   These have the locative singular in stressed **-у́**, e.g. **бре́де** but **в бреду́**. The locative of **вид** varies in different phrases, e.g. **в хоро́шем ви́де** *in good shape*, but **име́ть в виду́** *to mean, intend*.

цех and **строй** may have mobile stress—see §20a. In the sense of *perfume* the plural **духи́, духо́в** is used. Similarly the plural of **бег: бега́, бего́в** means '*races*'.

(ii) Polysyllabic masculine nouns with fixed stress are of the following types:

All masculine nouns with unstressed suffixes have fixed stress throughout. Only a few examples with various suffixes are given:

сто́лик	*little table*	ребёнок (ребёнка,	
ча́йник	*teapot*	pl. ребя́та)	*child*
пра́здник	*holiday*	жи́тель	*inhabitant*
ма́льчик	*boy*	писа́тель	*writer*
лётчик	*airman*	па́лец (па́льца)	*finger*
хло́пок (хло́пка)	*cotton*	па́харь	*ploughman*
посту́пок (посту́пка)	*act(ion)*	слу́чай	*case, occasion*

Учи́тель is an exception with mobile stress—see §20*a*.

Masculine nouns with unstressed prefixes have fixed stress throughout, e.g.

вопро́с	*question*	разгово́р	*conversation*
восто́к	*east*	разме́р	*size*
восто́рг	*rapture*	расска́з	*story*
заво́д	*works*	самова́р	*samovar*
зако́н	*law*	сове́т	*counsel, council*
отве́т	*answer*	сою́з	*union*
предме́т	*object, subject*	уда́р	*blow*
приме́р	*example*	успе́х	*success*

Other masculine nouns with fixed stress include:

бара́н	*ram*	наро́д	*people*
ве́тер (ве́тра:	loc.	обе́д	*dinner*
на ветру́)	*wind*	о́браз	*form, image*
во́здух	*air*	о́пыт	*experience*
вокза́л	*station*	оре́х	*nut*
во́рон	*raven*	о́тдых	*rest*
вы́ход	*exit*	се́вер	*north*
за́втрак	*breakfast*	сосе́д (pl.	
за́пад	*west*	сосе́ди)	*neighbour*
за́пах	*smell*	спо́соб	*way, method*
карма́н	*pocket*	стака́н	*glass*
лентя́й	*lazybones*	това́р	*wares*
ме́сяц	*moon, month*	трамва́й	*tramcar*
миллио́н	*million*	тума́н	*fog*
мо́лот	*hammer*	у́голь (у́гля)	*coal*
му́сор	*rubbish*	у́жин	*supper*

уро́к	*lesson*	цыга́н (pl. цыга́не,	
хозя́ин (pl. хозя́ева,		цыга́н)	*gipsy*
хозя́ев)	*host, landlord*		

О́браз in the meaning *ikon* has plural образа́ (see §20*a*).
У́голь may have mobile stress (see §24*c*).
Дя́дя *uncle* may have fixed stress, with plural дя́ди, дя́дей, but the forms дядья́, дядьёв also exist.

(iii) **Compound nouns as a rule have fixed stress**, even if the final element is a masculine noun with mobile stress, e.g. стол (стола́) *table*, but престо́л (престо́ла) *throne*; ум (ума́) *mind*, but ра́зум (ра́зума) *reason*; воз (pl. возы́) *cart, load*, but парово́з (pl. парово́зы) *locomotive*; друг (pl. друзья́) *friend*, but не́друг (pl. не́други) *enemy* (rhetorical); цвет (pl. цвета́) *colour*, but самоцве́т (pl. самоцве́ты) *semi-precious stone*; го́род (pl. города́) *town*, but при́город (pl. при́городы) *suburb*. There are exceptions however, e.g. о́стров (pl. острова́) *island* and полуо́стров (pl. полуострова́) *peninsula*; бог (pl. бо́ги, бого́в) *god* and полубо́г (pl. полубо́ги, полубого́в) *demigod*. Compound nouns in which the first element is an abbreviation retain the stress of the second element, e.g. врач (врача́) *doctor* —ветвра́ч (ветврача́) *vet* (from ветерина́рный врач); суд (суда́) *court*—нарсу́д (нарсуда́) *People's court* (from наро́дный суд).
Cf. also §§111, 112*c*, 112*d*.

(*e*) **Most foreign loan-words and 'international' words have fixed stress.** Examples are:

Masculine:

автомоби́ль	*motor-car*	пери́од	*period*
банк	*bank*	план	*plan*
биле́т	*ticket*	поэ́т	*poet*
га́лстук	*necktie*	проце́сс	*process*
геро́й	*hero*	результа́т	*result*
журна́л	*periodical*	рестора́н	*restaurant*
зал	*hall*	солда́т	*soldier*
класс	*class*	теа́тр	*theatre*
конве́рт	*envelope*	телефо́н	*telephone*
мета́лл	*metal*	факт	*fact*
моме́нт	*moment*	центр	*centre*
парк	*park*	шофёр	*driver*

See however note on borrowed nouns in **-ор** with mobile stress in §20*a*.

Feminine:

а́рмия	army	револю́ция	revolution
да́ма	lady	ста́нция	station
ка́рта	map	те́ма	theme, subject
ла́мпа	lamp	фо́рма	form
ма́сса	mass	фра́за	phrase
маши́на	machine	шко́ла	school
па́ртия	party	шту́ка	piece, article

Neuter: These are of course indeclinable, e.g.

бюро́	bureau	пальто́	overcoat
кино́	cinema	шоссе́	highway

NOUNS WITH MOBILE STRESS

§17. These show a variety of patterns:

(*a*) **Masculine nouns.** Apart from those with fixed stress mentioned above in §§16*a*, 16*d* and 16*e*, masculine nouns, especially those with only one syllable in the nom.sg., tend to have mobile stress, with the following patterns possible:

(i) Stress moves on to the case endings throughout sing. and pl. (see §19).

e.g. стол, стола́, столу́, etc., столы́, столо́в, стола́м, etc.

(ii) Stress in the singular is on the stem, but in the plural on the endings (see §20).

e.g. час, ча́са, ча́су, etc., часы́, часо́в, часа́м, etc.

All masc. nouns with nom.pl. in stressed -а́ have stress on the endings throughout the plural, e.g. дом—дома́.

(iii) Stress in the singular is on the stem, in the nominative plural is on the stem, but in all other cases in the plural on the endings (see §21).

e.g. гость, го́стя, го́стю, etc., го́сти, госте́й, гостя́м, etc.

(iv) Stress in both singular and plural is on the endings, except for the nominative plural. This is a very small group (see §24*c*).

e.g. конь, коня́, коню́, etc., ко́ни, коне́й, коня́м, etc.

The only general 'rule' which emerges is that for all masculine nouns having mobile stress, at least the oblique cases in the plural have stress on the endings (i.e. genitive, dative, instrumental and prepositional).

The only clear rule for knowing which masculine nouns have mobile stress is that masculine nouns with stressed suffixes in the nom.sg. have the accent moving on to the case endings throughout (see §19*b*).

(*b*) **Feminine nouns of the -a declension** with mobile accent all have the stress on the ending in the nom.sg., and conversely most feminine nouns with stress on the ending in the nom.sg. have mobile stress (see §16*b* for exceptions with fixed stress). The patterns are:

(i) Stress in the singular is on the endings, but in the plural on the stem (see §22).

e.g. жена́, жену́, жены́, etc., жёны, жён, жёнам, etc.

(ii) Stress in the singular is on the endings, except for the accusative (where it is on the stem), in the plural it is on the stem (see §23).

e.g. душа́, ду́шу, души́, etc., ду́ши, душ, ду́шам, etc.

(iii) Stress in both singular and plural is on the endings, except for the nominative plural, where it is on the stem (see §24).

e.g. волна́, волну́, волны́, etc., во́лны, волн, волна́м, etc.

(iv) Stress in both singular and plural is on the endings, except for the accusative singular and the nominative plural, where it is on the stem (see §25).

e.g. рука́, ру́ку, руки́, руке́, руко́й; pl. ру́ки, рук, рука́м, etc.

Patterns (iii)-(iv) are archaic survivals represented by a very limited number of frequently used nouns. They show some instability, particularly in the stress of the acc.sing. Pattern (ii) is in itself a symptom of instability, as it is a compromise between the very common pattern (i) and pattern (iv). Most grammarians do not in fact recognise it as a separate pattern. In general, stress on the stem in the acc.sing. of such feminine nouns is said to be gradually dying out. Many nouns are in a transitional state, being heard with stress either on the stem or the endings in the acc.sing. and the dat., instr. and prep.plural.

No general rule emerges, except that the nominative plural of nearly all feminine nouns has the accent on the stem, and that, apart from the limited number of very common nouns with stress moving on to the stem in the accusative singular (those in groups (ii) and (iv) above) stress in the singular of feminine nouns is fixed on the same syllable as that of the nominative singular.

(*c*) **Feminine nouns of the -ь declension** may have fixed stress (see §16*b*(ii) above) or mobile stress. Those with mobile stress have the accent on the stem in the singular and the nominative plural, and on the endings throughout the rest of the plural (cf. §21*b*).

Note that these conform to the general observation about the nominative plural in (*b*) above:

e.g. дверь, две́ри, две́рью; pl. две́ри, двере́й, дверя́м, etc.

Exceptions include **любо́вь** and the numerals like **пять**, with stress on the endings in all cases: **пяти́, пятью́** (see §19*d*).

Most longer feminine nouns, and nearly all with abstract suffixes, have fixed stress (see §§16*a*(ii), 16*b*, 16*c*).

(*d*) **Neuter nouns** of two syllables (and some with more) have two patterns of mobile stress:

(i) Stress in the singular is on the stem, in the plural on the endings (see §20*b*).

     e.g. **сло́во, сло́ва, сло́ву,** etc., **слова́, слов, слова́м,** etc.

(ii) Stress in the singular is on the endings, in the plural on the stem (see §22*b*).

     e.g. **окно́, окна́, окну́,** etc., **о́кна, о́кон, о́кнам,** etc.

There are a few isolated exceptions, e.g. **у́хо** (see §21*c* below) and **плечо́** and **крыльцо́** (see §24*b* below) and some disyllabic nouns with fixed stress (see §16*b*(iii) above).

Apart from these exceptions, however, it is a fairly reliable rule that **for most neuter nouns of two syllables, the stress alternates between the singular and the plural**, i.e. if the accent is on the stem in the singular it will be on the endings in the plural, and vice versa.

Most longer neuter nouns, and all those with abstract suffixes, have fixed stress (see §§16*a*(iii), 16*c*(ii)).

§18. All the above patterns of mobile stress involve the accent moving on to or off the case endings. In some nouns, however, stress moves only within the stem, e.g.

     граждани́н, pl. **гра́ждане** and a few others of this type (see §10*d*). **о́зеро,** pl. **озёра; зна́мя,** pl. **знамёна** and others of this type (see §20*b*).

Also **Госпо́дь** *Lord*, with stress moving on to the first syllable in all other cases, e.g. gen./acc. **Го́спода,** vocative **Го́споди!**

Neuter nouns in **-ство** with stress on the endings move the accent on to the last syllable of the stem in the gen.pl. with zero ending, e.g. **существо́** *being*—**суще́ств**. Otherwise stress is fixed in these.

Stress frequently moves within the stem in conjunction with the above patterns, especially in forming the genitive plural with zero ending of neuter and feminine nouns, e.g.

     дере́вня, pl. **дере́вни, дереве́нь, деревня́м**

See §§20*b*, 21*b*, 22, 23, 24.

Diagram of stress patterns in nouns

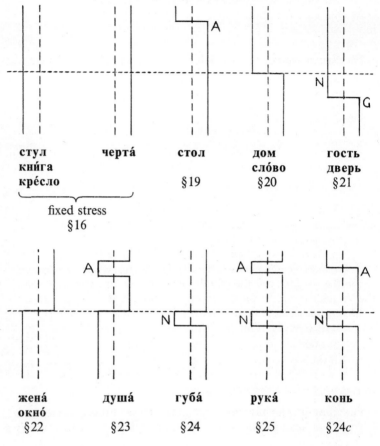

The vertical dotted line marks the division between the stem (to the left) and the endings (to the right). The horizontal dotted line marks the division between the singular (above) and plural (below). The heavy line marks the position of stress. N (nominative), A (accusative) and G (genitive) have been marked where necessary. For example in **стол** stress is on the stem in the nominative singular, but on the endings in all other cases. The order of cases is nom., acc., gen., dat., instr., prep.

In §§24 and 25 and in neuter nouns in §20 stress is on the stem also in the genitive plural (**слов, губ, рук**), but this form has been ignored, as it has zero ending and does not contribute anything significant to the pattern.

NOUNS GROUPED ACCORDING TO STRESS PATTERNS

§19. Accent moves on to the case endings throughout singular and plural in a large number of masculine nouns.

Он взял кни́гу со стола́.	*He took the book from the table.*
Ся́дьте побли́же к столу́.	*Sit nearer the table.*
Она́ сиде́ла за столо́м.	*She was sitting at the table.*
В ко́мнате стоя́т столы́.	*There are tables in the room.*
Всего́ пять столо́в.	*There are five tables altogether.*
На стола́х лежа́т кни́ги.	*There are books lying on the tables.*

(*a*) Monosyllabic nouns with stressed endings in all cases include:

враг	*enemy*	поп	*priest*
врач	*doctor*	пруд†	*pond*
грех	*sin*	скот	*cattle*
гриб	*mushroom*	слон	*elephant*
двор	*yard*	стих	*verse*
Днепр	*Dnieper*	стол	*table*
ключ	*key; spring*	суд	*court*
крест	*cross*	труд	*labour*
луч	*ray*	ум	*mind*
мяч	*ball*	хвост	*tail*
нож	*knife*	холм	*hill*
Пётр (Петра́)	*Peter*	дождь	*rain*
плащ	*raincoat*	Кремль	*Kremlin*
плод	*fruit*	рубль	*rouble*
полк†	*regiment*	царь	*Tsar*

Also **путь (пути́, путём)** *way*.

Nouns with fugitive vowel can be grouped here, as their stems become monosyllabic in declension even if the nom.sing. is disyllabic:

день (дня)	*day*	ого́нь (огня́)	*fire*
ковёр (ковра́)	*carpet*	орёл (орла́)	*eagle*
козёл (козла́)	*goat*	осёл (осла́)	*donkey*
котёл (котла́)	*boiler*	пень (пня)	*tree-stump*
лев (льва)	*lion*	рот (рта)†	*mouth*
лёд (льда)†	*ice*	сон (сна)	*sleep*
лён (льна)	*flax*	у́гол (угла́)†	*corner*
лоб (лба)†	*forehead*	у́зел (узла́)	*bundle*
овёс (овса́)	*oats*		

† These have the locative singular in stressed -у́, e.g. **Он говори́л о льде** but **Он стоя́л на льду.**

Less essential monosyllabic nouns with stressed endings throughout include:

блин	*pancake*	плющ	*ivy*
боб	*bean*	пост	*fast*
бык	*bull*	пост†	*post*
винт	*screw*	руль	*rudder, steering-wheel*
вол	*ox*	серп	*sickle*
вред	*harm*	сноп	*sheaf*
грач	*rook*	ствол	*trunk, gun-barrel*
дрозд	*thrush*	столб	*pillar*
ёж (ежа́)	*hedgehog*	стыд	*shame*
жук	*beetle*	ткач	*weaver*
клоп	*bedbug*	туз	*ace*
кот	*tom-cat*	холст	*canvas*
куст	*bush*	шест	*pole*
меч	*sword*	штык	*bayonet*
плот	*raft*	щит	*shield*

(*b*) Polysyllabic nouns masculine with stressed endings. There is
one good rule: **all masculine nouns with stressed suffixes in the nominative singular have stress on the endings in all other cases.** (The suffixes
-ан, -ор, -ёр, -изм, -ист and **-аж** are exceptions to this rule.) (Cf.
§10.) Only a few examples with various suffixes are given:

-ик

воротни́к	*collar*	мужи́к	*peasant*
грузови́к	*lorry*	стари́к	*old man*
дневни́к	*diary*	учени́к	*pupil*
матери́к	*continent*	часовщи́к	*watchmaker*

e.g. Я зна́ю э́того ученика́. Все ученики́ хоро́шие.

In таджи́к *a Tadjik*, **-ик** is not a suffix, and stress is fixed.

-ок

звоно́к (звонка́)	*bell*	плато́к (платка́)	*cloth, kerchief*
кусо́к (куска́)	*piece*	потоло́к (потолка́)	*ceiling*
мешо́к (мешка́)	*bag*	чуло́к (чулка́,	*stocking*
кошелёк (кошелька́)	*purse*	g.pl. чуло́к)	

There are a few exceptions in which stress moves on to the stem in
the plural, e.g. глазо́к *eye* (dimin.), gen. sing. глазка́, pl. гла́з-
ки, гла́зок, гла́зкам; in the meanings *eye of a potato* and *peep-
hole* however the pl. is глазки́, глазко́в. Similarly рожо́к,
dimin. of рог *horn*: ро́жки, ро́жек *horns of an animal*, рожки́,
рожко́в *musical instruments*.

† See footnote on previous page.

-éц

дворе́ц (дворца́)	palace	оте́ц (отца́)	father
коне́ц (конца́)	end	мертве́ц (мертвеца́)	corpse
купе́ц (купца́)	merchant		

-а́к

дура́к	fool	моря́к	sailor
каза́к	Cossack	чуда́к	eccentric
пиджа́к	jacket		

Поля́к *a Pole* is an exception with stress fixed on stem throughout.
Каза́к formerly had stress on the stem in the plural: каза́ки, but
   казаки́, казако́в is now normal.

-еж/-ёж

рубе́ж	border(line)	платёж (платежа́)	payment
паде́ж	case (gramm.)		

-а́ч

бога́ч	rich man	скрипа́ч	violinist

-и́ч

кирпи́ч	brick	москви́ч	Muscovite
Фоми́ч	patronymic from Фома́	Thomas	
Ильи́ч	patronymic from Илья́	Elias	

-у́н

бегу́н	runner	горбу́н	hunchback

-а́рь

слова́рь	dictionary	фона́рь	lantern, street-lamp

-у́х

пасту́х	shepherd	пету́х	cock

Other masculine nouns with stress moving on to the endings
throughout all cases include:

бага́ж	baggage	рыча́г	lever
башма́к	shoe	сапо́г (g.pl. сапо́г)	boot
жени́х	fiancé, bridegroom	солове́й (соловья́)	
каранда́ш	pencil		nightingale
кома́р	gnat	сунду́к	trunk, chest
кора́бль	ship	таба́к	tobacco
коро́ль	king	топо́р	axe
пау́к	spider	утю́г	(smoothing) iron
монасты́рь	monastery	четве́рг	Thursday
посо́л (посла́)	ambassador	эта́ж	storey
рука́в (pl. рукава́)	sleeve	язы́к	tongue, language
руче́й (ручья́)	stream		

and some of the names of the months with soft endings: **янва́рь** (**января́**), **февра́ль, сентя́брь, октя́брь, ноя́брь, дека́брь** (but not **апре́ль, ию́нь, ию́ль** which, like **ма́рт, май, а́вгуст** have fixed stress).

Лист in the sense *sheet* (*of paper, etc.*) has this pattern (pl. **листы́, листо́в**), but in the sense *leaf*, while the accent falls on the endings in the singular, it is on the stem in the plural—**ли́стья, ли́стьев**.

(*c*) **Христо́с** *Christ* may be grouped here, as it loses the Greek nominative ending **-ос** and has the accent on the endings in all other cases: **Христа́, Христу́, Христо́м, о Христе́**.

(*d*) A few feminine nouns can conveniently be grouped here, although they do not conform completely to this rule, namely: **любо́вь** *love* (gen., dat. and prep.sg. **любви́**; instr. **любо́вью**), **ложь** *lie* (gen., dat., prep. **лжи**; instr. **ло́жью**), **Русь** *Russia* (**Руси́**; instr. **Ру́сью**), **Пермь** (**Перми́**) *Perm*. The numerals which decline as feminine nouns of the **-ь** declension conform completely, e.g. **пять, пяти́, пятью́**, but see the section on numerals, §50*c*.

§20. Accent in the singular is on the stem, in the plural on the endings in a large number of masculine and neuter nouns.

Четы́ре сло́ва	*Four words*
Вы найдёте все слова́ в словаре́.	*You will find all the words in the dictionary.*
Одни́м сло́вом, э́то невоз-мо́жно.	*In short, it's impossible.*
Други́ми слова́ми, вы не хоти́те.	*In other words, you don't want to.*
В э́том сло́ве пять букв.	*There are five letters in this word.*
В его́ слова́х бы́ло что́-то стра́нное.	*There was something strange in what he said.*

(*a*) Masculine: These, chiefly monosyllabic, masculine nouns form a very homogeneous group. They tend to have in common, in addition to this stress pattern (singular on stem, plural on endings), some of the three following characteristics, marked respectively [1], [2], [3]:

1. Nominative plural in stressed **-а́** (cf. §17*a*(ii)).

2. Locative singular in stressed **-у́** (along with a normally stressed prepositional in **-е**), e.g.
   Он говори́л о своём са́де. *He was speaking about his garden.*
   Мы сиде́ли в саду́. *We were sitting in the garden.*

3. Sometimes a genitive singular in **-у** (generally as a partitive and in fixed phrases, e.g. **кило́ сы́ру** *a kilogram of cheese*; **он вы́шел из до́му** *he left the house*). See also §106*a*(vii).

The locative in -ý is sometimes not essential in modern Russian, and in that case has been marked [2]. The partitive in -y is also not always essential in modern Russian.

The following monosyllables belong to this group:

бал[2]	*ball*	пол[2,3]	*floor*
бой[2,3]	*battle*	раз[3](g.pl. **раз**)	*time*
бок[1,2,3]	*side*	рай[2]	*Paradise*
бор[2]	*pine forest*	рог[1]	*horn*
век[1,(2),3]	*century, age*	род[(2),3]	*kind* (see below)
верх[2,3]	*top*	рой[2]	*swarm*
воз[2,3]	*cart, load*	ряд[2,3]	*row*
глаз[1,2,3] (g.pl.		сад[2]	*garden*
глаз)	*eye*	сорт[1]	*sort, grade*
гроб[2]	*coffin*	снег[1,(2),3]	*snow*
дар	*gift*	стог[1,(2)]	*haystack*
долг[2,3]	*debt, duty*	строй[2]	*rank, formation*
дом[1,(2),3]	*house*	сын (pl. **сыновья́, сыновéй,**	
друг (pl. **друзья́, друзéй,**		**сыновья́м**) *son*	
друзья́м) *friend*		сыр[3]	*cheese*
дуб[2]	*oak*	счёт[(1),2,3]	*account*(see below)
дым[(2),3]	*smoke*	цвет[(1),2,3]	*flower, colour* (see
зад	*hindquarters*		below)
князь (pl. **князья́,**		том[1]	*volume*
князéй) *prince*		ус	*moustache*
край[1,2,3]	*edge*	хлеб[(1)]	*bread, corn* (see
круг[2,3]	*circle*		below)
ла́герь[1]	*camp* (see below)	ход[(2),3]	*movement, 'go'*
лес[1,2,3]	*forest*	чай[3]	*tea*
луг[1,2]	*meadow*	час[2,3]	*hour* (see below)
мех[1,(2,3)]	*fur* (see below)	чин	*rank*
мир[3]	*world*	шаг[(2),3]	*step* (see below)
мост[2,3]	*bridge*	шар	*sphere* (see below)
муж (pl. **мужья́,**		шёлк[1] (pl. **шелка́**) *silk*	
мужéй) *husband*		шкаф[2]	*cupboard*
нос[2,3]	*nose*		

След *footprint, trace* almost conforms to this pattern, but has the accent on the ending in the gen.sg., e.g. **без следа́** *without trace*.

Four of these nouns have the stress on the ending of the genitive singular after the numerals **два, три, четы́ре** only. They are: **ряд, час, шаг** and **шар**. For instance **до ча́са** *before one o'clock*, but **два часа́, три часа́, четы́ре часа́** *two hours/o'clock*, etc.; **э́того ря́да** *of this row*, but **два ряда́**, etc. In the sense *spheres* or *balloons* **шар** has normal stress after these numerals, e.g. **два ша́ра**, but in the sense *balls* it has final stress: **три шара́**.

Polysyllabic nouns with stress on the stem in the singular, on the endings in the plural include:

а́дрес[1]	address	по́вар[1]	cook
бе́рег[1,2]	bank, shore	по́езд[1]	train
ве́чер[1]	evening	по́яс[1]	belt
го́лос[1]	voice	сто́рож[1]	watchman
го́род[1]	town	учи́тель[1]	teacher(see below)
господи́н (pl. господа́, госпо́д,		хо́лод[1,(2,3)]	cold
господа́м) *Mr, gentleman*		че́реп[1]	skull
ко́локол[1]	bell		
но́мер[1]	number	дире́ктор[1]	director
о́браз[1]	ikon (see below)	до́ктор[1]	doctor
о́стров[1]	island	кондуктор[1]	conductor
па́рус[1]	sail	ма́стер[1]	foreman
па́спорт[1]	passport	профе́ссор[1]	professor

N.B. Many borrowed nouns ending in -ор like the last five in this list have the plural in stressed -а́, and in general the tendency to make plurals of this type (and therefore having this stress pattern) is strong in colloquial Russian where 'incorrectly' such forms as **офицера́, инженера́, лектора́, трактора́, воза́, волоса́,** and even **месяца́** occur along with the accepted forms **офице́ры, инжене́ры, ле́кторы, тра́кторы, возы́, во́лосы, ме́сяцы**. For **цех** *workshop* both **це́хи** (with fixed stress) and **цеха́** (with stressed endings in the plural) are used.

Some pairs of homonyms are distinguished in the plural by these endings and therefore incidentally by the stress, e.g.

хле́бы	loaves	хлеба́	corn, grain
ме́хи	bellows	меха́	furs
цвето́к—цветы́	flower(s)	цвет—цвета́	colour(s)
про́воды	seeing-off, send-off	провода́	wires
про́пуски	omissions	пропуска́	passes, permits

Счёты is the plural of **счёт** mainly in figurative fixed phrases (e.g. **своди́ть ста́рые счёты** *to pay off old scores*) and is also the word for *abacus, counting frame*, while the ordinary plural for *accounts* is **счета́**.

The ordinary plural of **учи́тель** *teacher* is **учителя́**, but **учи́тели** is used for *teachers of a doctrine, philosophers*. **Лагеря́** is the normal plural for *camps* in a literal sense—military, boys' camps, but in a figurative sense, e.g. *two hostile camps* the form **ла́гери** is used.

The normal plural of **сын** *son* is **сыновья́**, but in a figurative sense, e.g. *Sons of the Fatherland* the form **сыны́, сыно́в** is used. As the plural of **год** *year* both **го́ды** and **года́** are used indiscriminately, except that in naming a more or less definite period of history **го́ды** is always used, e.g. **шестидеся́тые го́ды** *the sixties*, **го́ды Револю́ции** *the years of the Revolution*. The plural of **род** *kind* is **роды́, родо́в**, but the word for *childbirth* is **ро́ды, ро́дов**.

(*b*) Neuter: Many common neuter nouns have the accent on the stem in the singular, on the endings in the plural (cf. §17*d*), e.g.

во́йско	*army*	**се́рдце** (g.pl. **серде́ц**)	*heart*
де́ло	*affair*	**сло́во**	*word*
ле́то	*summer*	**ста́до**	*flock*
ма́сло	*butter, oil*	**су́дно** (pl. **суда́,**	
ме́сто	*place*	**судо́в**)	*ship, vessel*
мо́ре	*sea*	**те́ло**	*body*
не́бо (pl. **небеса́,**		**зе́ркало** (g.pl. **зе́ркал**	
небе́с)	*sky, heavens*	or **зерка́л**)	*mirror*
по́ле	*field*	**о́блако** (g.pl.	
пра́во	*right, law*	**облако́в**)	*cloud*

Note however: **о́зеро** *lake*, pl. **озёра**, gen.pl. **озёр**; and **де́рево** *tree*, pl. **дере́вья, дере́вьев** (cf. **перо́** and others, §22*b*).

Neuter nouns ending in **-мя** have this stress pattern (except **зна́мя** *banner*), e.g. **вре́мя, вре́мени** *time*, pl. **времена́, времён, времена́м**. Similarly **и́мя** *name*, **пле́мя** *tribe*, **се́мя** *seed* (with gen.pl. **семя́н**), and **стре́мя** *stirrup* (with gen.pl. **стремя́н**). **Зна́мя**, gen. **зна́мени** has plural **знамёна, знамён, знамёнам**. (The four other nouns of this declension have no plural forms: **бре́мя** *burden*, **вы́мя** *udder*, **пла́мя** *flame*, **те́мя** *crown of the head*.)

§21. Accent in the singular is on the stem, in the nominative plural on the stem, but in all other cases in the plural on the endings.

У нас вчера́ бы́ли го́сти.	*We had guests yesterday.*
Она́ посмотре́ла на го́стя.	*She looked at the guest.*
Он вёз госте́й со ста́нции.	*He brought the guests from the station.*
Хозя́ин предложи́л го́стю вы́пить.	*The host offered his guest a drink.*
Хозя́ин предложи́л гостя́м вы́пить.	*The host offered his guests a drink.*
Они́ говори́ли о своём го́сте.	*They were speaking about their guest.*
В январе́ он был у нас в гостя́х.	*He stayed with us in January.*

(a) Masculine: A limited number of masculine nouns with hard endings and several with soft endings have this pattern:

бог	god	зуб	tooth (see below)
волк	wolf	пол	sex
во́лос (g.pl.	hair	слог	syllable
волос)		фронт	front (of battle)
вор	thief		
(loc.sg. в году́)	year	чёрт (pl. че́рти, чертёй,	
(see also note to §20a)		чертя́м)	devil

The teeth of a *comb*, etc. are зу́бья, зу́бьев or зубцы́, зубцо́в.

го́лубь	pigeon	ко́рень (ко́рня)	root
гость	guest	ле́бедь	swan
гусь	goose	ло́коть (ло́ктя)	elbow
зверь	animal	но́готь (но́гтя)	finger-nail
	(see §26)	па́рень (па́рня)	fellow, lad
ка́мень (ка́мня)	stone	сте́бель (сте́бля)	stem, stalk
ко́готь (ко́гтя)	claw		

The plural коре́нья, коре́ньев is used in the sense of *root veget-ables*, and the plural каме́нья, каме́ньев *stones* is also found.

(b) Feminine: Only one common noun of the -a declension has this pattern, i.e. дере́вня, дере́вни; дере́вни, дереве́нь, деревня́м *village*.

A considerable number of feminine nouns of the -ь declension, however, have the accent in the singular and nominative plural on the stem, otherwise in the plural on the endings. (Others have fixed stress; see §§16b(ii), 16c.)

e.g. дверь, две́ри, etc. — две́ри, дверёй, дверя́м.

Several of these have the ending of the locative singular stressed, e.g. Мы говори́ли о сте́пи *We were speaking about the steppe*, but Они́ жи́ли в степи́ *They lived on the steppe*. Such nouns are marked †.

бровь†	brow	ось†	axle
весть	news	печь†	stove
ветвь	branch	речь	speech
вещь	thing	роль	role
власть	power	са́ни (pl. only)	sledge
грудь†	breast (see below)	се́ни (pl. only)	vestibule
дверь† (see §26		сеть(†)	net
for instr.pl.)	door	смерть	death
кость(†)	bone	соль	salt
мышь	mouse	степь†	steppe
ночь†	night	страсть	passion

тень†	shadow	пло́щадь	square
треть	third	по́весть	story
цепь†на цепи́	chain	ска́терть	tablecloth
часть	part	сте́пень	degree
щель†	crack, chink	це́рковь	church (see below)
ло́шадь (instr.pl. лошадьми́, see §26)	horse	че́тверть	quarter
о́бласть	province	ше́рсть	wool
о́чередь	turn, queue		

(в тени́)

Це́рковь declines as follows: gen., dat., prep.sing.: це́ркви, instr. sing. церко́вью, plural: це́ркви, церкве́й, церква́м.

The gen.sing. of грудь may also have the accent on the ending, and with prepositions the ending of the dat.sing. is always stressed, e.g. по груди́, к груди́.

A few nouns in -ость have this pattern, viz. кре́пость *fort*, но́вость *news*, ско́рость *speed*. (Otherwise nouns with this suffix have fixed stress, cf. §16c(i).)

Мать and дочь also have this pattern: мать, ма́тери — ма́тери, матере́й, матеря́м, матеря́ми. Дочь has the instrumental plural дочерьми́ (see below §26).

(c) Neuter: The two nouns у́хо *ear* and о́ко *eye* have this pattern, with plural у́ши, уше́й, уша́м; о́чи, оче́й, оча́м.

§22. Accent in the singular is on the endings, in the plural on the stem, in many feminine and neuter nouns.

США о́чень больша́я страна́.	The U.S.A. is a very big country.
Я хорошо́ зна́ю э́ту страну́.	I know that country well.
Они́ из далёкой страны́.	They are from a distant country.
Стра́ны Евро́пы.	The countries of Europe.
Тру́дно е́здить по э́той стране́.	It is difficult to travel in that country.
Он путеше́ствовал по мно́гим стра́нам.	He has travelled in many countries.
Вы бы́ли в э́той стране́?	Have you been in that country?
Он побыва́л во мно́гих стра́нах.	He *has been* in many countries.

(a) Feminine:

беда́	misfortune	вина́	fault, blame
вдова́	widow	война́	war
верста́ (pl. вёрсты)	verst (see below)	волна́ (see also §24a)	wave
весна́ (pl. вёсны, вёсен)	Spring	глава́	chapter
		гроза́	thunderstorm

дыра́	hole	плита́	slab; cooker
жена́ (pl. жёны)	wife	пчела́ (pl.	
звезда́ (pl.		пчёлы)	bee
звёзды)	star	сестра́ (pl. сёстры,	
змея́ (g.pl. змей)	snake	сестёр)	sister
игла́ (g.pl. игл)	needle	скала́	rock
игра́	game	слуга́ (masc.)	servant
изба́ (acc.sg. избу́		сосна́ (g.pl.	
ог избу)	peasant house	со́сен)	pine
коза́	goat	среда́	surroundings
коса́ (acc. косу́			(see also §25)
ог ко́су)	scythe (cf. §23)	страна́	country
лиса́	fox	стрела́	arrow
луна́	moon	струна́	string
метла́ (pl. мётлы,		судьба́ (g.pl.	fate (see below)
мётел)	broom, besom	су́деб)	
нужда́	need	толпа́ (g.pl.	
овца́ (g.pl.		толп)	crowd
ове́ц)	sheep	трава́	grass
орда́	horde	труба́	pipe, trumpet
оса́	wasp	тюрьма́ (g.pl.	
пила́	saw	тю́рем)	prison

(margin note: ОВЦЫ)

Верста́ sometimes has acc.sing. вёрсту (giving rise to phrases with stress on the preposition, e.g. за́ версту or за версту́, cf. §106) and in the prepositional pl., as well as the normal form, e.g. исчисле́ние в вёрстах *counting in versts*, has верста́х in such phrases as они живу́т в двух верста́х *they live within two versts from here.*

(margin note: КИЛОМЕТР is much more common nowadays)

Note the abnormal stress in one phrase with судьба́: каки́ми судьба́ми!? *by what strange chance!?*

Several nouns ending in -ота́, -ина́ and other suffixes have this pattern, with the accent moving on to the second last syllable of the suffix in the plural: красота́ — красо́ты, красо́т, красо́там, etc. e.g.

высота́	height	хло́поты, хлопо́т,	
кислота́	acid(ity)	хло́потам (no sing.)	trouble, fuss
красота́	beauty	величина́	magnitude, quantity
сирота́	orphan	глубина́	depth
широта́	width, latitude	стрекоза́	dragonfly
колбаса́	sausage		

(margin note: глубины)

A few other nouns have this pattern, except that in the gen.pl. the accent is on the ending, e.g. семья́, семьи́ *family*, pl. се́мьи, семе́й, се́мьям. Similarly свинья́ *pig* and судья́ (masc.) *judge.*

(b) Neuter: Many common two-syllable neuter nouns have the accent in the singular on the endings, in the plural on the stem (cf. §17d).

бедро́ (pl. бё́дра, бё́дер)	thigh, hip
бревно́ (pl. брё́вна, брё́вен)	log
ведро́ (pl. вё́дра, вё́дер)	bucket
весло́ (pl. вё́сла, вё́сел)	oar
вино́ *(pl. ви́на)*	wine
гнездо́ (pl. гнё́зда)	nest
зерно́ (pl. зё́рна, зё́рен)	grain
кольцо́ (g.pl. коле́ц)	ring
копьё́ (pl. ко́пья, ко́пий, ко́пьям)	spear
лицо́	face, person
окно́ (g.pl. о́кон)	window
письмо́ (g.pl. пи́сем)	letter
ребро́ (pl. рё́бра, рё́бер)	rib
ружьё́ (pl. ру́жья, ру́жей)	gun
седло́ (pl. сё́дла, сё́дел)	saddle
село́ (pl. сё́ла)	village
стекло́ (pl. стё́кла, стё́кол)	glass, pane
сукно́ (g.pl. су́кон)	cloth
число́ (g.pl. чи́сел)	number, date
ядро́ (g.pl. я́дер)	kernel, nucleus
яйцо́ (pl. я́йца, яи́ц, я́йцам)	egg
пятно́ (g.pl. пя́тен)	spot, stain

A few irregular plurals occur here, e.g. перо́ — пе́рья, пе́рьев, пе́рьям *feather, pen.* Similarly крыло́ *wing;* звено́ *link;* and дно *bottom* with plural до́нья, до́ньев.

Also some nouns of three syllables:

волокно́ (pl. воло́кна, воло́кон)	fibre
колесо́ (pl. колё́са, колё́с)	wheel
полотно́ (pl. поло́тна, поло́тен)	linen
ремесло́ (pl. ремё́сла, ремё́сел)	trade, craft
решето́ (pl. решё́та, решё́т)	sieve

§23. **Accent in the singular is on the endings** except for the accusative singular (where it is on the stem), **in the plural on the stem,** in a few feminine nouns only,

e.g. душа́, ду́шу, души́, etc. — ду́ши, душ, ду́шам, etc.

Similarly:

вода́	water	коса́	plait, tress
душа́	soul		(cf. §22a)
земля́ (g.pl. земе́ль)	earth, land	спина́	back
		цена́	price
зима́	winter		

це́ны

Note, however, the stress on the ending in the phrase говори́ть по душа́м *to have a heart-to-heart talk.*

§24. Accent in both singular and plural is on the endings, except for the nominative plural where it is on the stem, in a number of feminine and some other nouns,

e.g. губа́, губу́, губы́ — гу́бы, губ, губа́м, *etc.*

(*a*) Feminine:

блоха́	*flea*	слеза́ (pl. слёзы)	*tear*
волна́ (see also §22*a*)	*wave*	строка́	*line*
губа́	*lip*	строфа́	*stanza*
свеча́ (gen.pl. свече́й)	*candle*	тропа́	*path*
борозда́ (pl. бо́розды, боро́зд, борозда́м)			*furrow*
де́ньги (no sing.), де́нег, деньга́м			*money*
ноздря́ (pl. но́здри, ноздре́й, ноздря́м)			*nostril*
полоса́ (pl. по́лосы, поло́с, полоса́м)			*stripe, strip*
простыня́ (pl. про́стыни, просты́нь, простыня́м)			*bed-sheet*
сковорода́ (pl. ско́вороды, сковоро́д, сковорода́м)			*frying-pan*

The accusative singular of **строка́, тропа́, борозда́, полоса́** may also be stressed on the stem: **стро́ку, тро́пу, бо́розду, по́лосу** (cf. §25).

По́хороны (f.pl.) *a funeral*, with no singular forms, belongs here—**похоро́н** (gen.), **похорона́м**.

(*b*) Two common neuter nouns have this pattern:

крыльцо́, крыльца́ — кры́льца, крыле́ц, крыльца́м   *porch*
плечо́, плеча́ — пле́чи, плеч, плеча́м   *shoulder*

(*c*) A few masculine nouns can be grouped here, since they have the accent moving on to the case endings except in the nominative plural, e.g. **конь, коня́, коню́ — ко́ни, коне́й, коня́м** *horse*.

Similarly **гвоздь** *nail* and **червь** *worm*.

У́голь *coal* may have this pattern, or else stress fixed on the first syllable throughout: **угля́, углю́, углём — у́гли, угле́й,** or **у́гля, у́глю, у́глем — у́гли, у́глей.** Two meanings are differentiated in the plural: various *types of coal*, with stress on stem: **у́глей**, etc., and *pieces of charcoal*, with stress on endings: **угле́й**, etc.

§25. Accent in both singular and plural is on the endings, except for the accusative singular and the nominative plural, where it is on the stem, in feminine nouns only, including a number of very common ones, e.g. **рука́, ру́ку, руки́ — ру́ки, рук, рука́м.** Similarly:

гора́	*mountain*	рука́	*hand, arm*
доска́ (g.pl. досо́к)	*board*	среда́	*Wednesday* (see also §22*a*)
нога́	*foot, leg*	стена́	*wall*
пора́	*time*	щека́ (pl. щёки)	*cheek*
река́	*river* (see below)		

борода́ (бо́роду; pl. бо́роды, боро́д)   *beard*
голова́ (го́лову; pl. го́ловы, голо́в)   *head*
сторона́ (сто́рону; pl. сто́роны, сторо́н)   *side*

Река́ also occurs with accent on the endings throughout the singular and on the stem throughout the plural: реку́ — ре́кам, etc.

The 'incorrect' stress of the gen.sing. which occurs in some phrases with numerals, e.g. по о́бе сто́роны, о́бе щёки, is in fact much more common than the 'correct' forms with стороны́, щеки́.

§26. Aberrant stress: locative singular in -у́ and -и́, and instrumental plural in -ьми́.

(*a*) The loc.sg. in stressed -у́ occurs in a considerable number of masculine nouns irrespective of their basic stress pattern. Some of them have stress fixed on the stem apart from this form, e.g. бег, о беге́, but на бегу́ (cf. §16*d*(i), (ii)). Others have stress on the stem throughout the singular, except for this ending, and mobile stress in the plural, e.g. сад, о са́де, в саду́, pl. сады́ (cf. §20*a*) and год, о го́де, в году́, pl. го́ды, годо́в (cf. §21*a*). It also occurs in nouns which move the stress on to all case endings, e.g. у́гол, об угле́, в углу́ (cf. §19*a*).

(*b*) The loc.sg. in stressed -и́ occurs in some feminine nouns of the -ь declension. Some have stress on the stem apart from this, e.g. кровь, кро́ви, в крови́ (cf. §16*b*(ii)); others have mobile stress in the plural, e.g. дверь, о две́ри, в двери́, pl. две́ри, двере́й (cf. §21*b*).

(*c*) The plural nouns лю́ди *people* and де́ти *children* have the accent on the ending in the genitive/accusative and the instrumental (in -ьми), but otherwise on the stem: лю́ди, люде́й, лю́дям, людьми́, о лю́дях.

Several nouns listed in §21 have this alternative form of ending in the instrumental singular, e.g. зверь — зверьми́ or normally зверя́ми; дверь — дверя́ми or дверьми́; ло́шадь — normally лошадьми́ (but лошадя́ми is permissible); дочь — дочерьми́ (and, colloquially, дочеря́ми).

CHAPTER 3

ADJECTIVES

LONG FORM

§27. In the long form of the adjective the accent is always fixed throughout on the same syllable as in the masculine singular, e.g.

хоро́ший, хоро́шая, хоро́шее, хоро́шие   *good*
плохо́й, плоха́я, плохо́е, плохи́е   *bad*

Adjectives having stress on the endings in the long form are listed after those with stress on the stem in §§ 37, 38, 40, and in §§ 139, 143-47.

Also stressed on the endings are the adjectival pronouns како́й, тако́й, друго́й, ино́й, любо́й; and the ordinal numerals второ́й, шесто́й, седьмо́й, восьмо́й and сороково́й.

§28. There are a few pairs of adjectives differentiated in the nominative singular by stress, e.g. чу́дный *wonderful* and чудно́й *strange, odd*; стра́стный *passionate* and страстно́й *of Christ's Passion* (as in Страстна́я Неде́ля *Passion Week*); the adjective from у́голь *coal* is у́гольный but from у́гол *corner, angle* — уго́льный.

§29. Note the characteristic stressed syllable with certain adjectival suffixes:

With the following suffixes the accent is always on the stem (usually on the syllable before the suffix):

-енький/-онький. Such diminutives as ма́ленький, но́венький always have the stress on the stem even if the original adjective has stressed endings, e.g. голубо́й — голу́бенький; молодо́й — моло́денький. But often in the adverbs derived from them the accent moves on to the suffix, e.g. хоро́шенький — хоро-ше́нько; ти́хенький ог ти́хонький—тихо́нько, тихо́хонько.

-еский   e.g. дру́жеский *friendly*

-очный   e.g. оши́бочный *mistaken*

-шний: with this suffix the stress of the basic word is retained, e.g. вчера́шний *yesterday's*, сего́дняшний *today's*

The following suffixes are always stressed:

-и́тый   e.g. знамени́тый *famous*

-ови́тый   e.g. делови́тый *businesslike*

-а́стый   e.g. зуба́стый *having large teeth*

-ова́тый   e.g. винова́тый *guilty*, красова́тый *reddish*

-áльный   e.g. **нормáльный** *normal*
-óнный   e.g. **райóнный** *regional*, **сенсациóнный** *sensational*
-и́вный   e.g. **наи́вный** *naive*, **субъекти́вный** *subjective*
-áйный, -éйный, -и́йный, -óйный, e.g. **семéйный** *family*,
       парти́йный *party*
-áтельный/-и́тельный, e.g. **замечáтельный** *remarkable*,
       удиви́тельный *surprising*
-и́ческий   e.g. **истори́ческий** *historical*, **коммунисти́ческий**
       Communist
-áйский, -éйский, -и́йский, -óйский, e.g. **европéйский** *Euro-*
       pean, **росси́йский** *Russian*
-áнский/-я́нский   e.g. **республикáнский** *republican*
-áторский   e.g. **орáторский** *oratorical*
-и́стский   e.g. **большеви́стский** *Bolshevik*
-áтельский/-и́тельский   e.g. **учи́тельский** *teachers'*
-у́чий   e.g. **могу́чий** *mighty*
-éлый   e.g. **престарéлый** *aged*

With other suffixes stress may be on the stem or the suffix, and no easy rule applies, e.g.

сóбственный	*own*	but	**обыкновéнный**	*usual*
вéжливый	*polite*	but	**справедли́вый**	*just*
жéнский	*female*	but	**мужскóй**	*male*

рóзовый *pink* — **фруктóвый** *fruit* — **мировóй** *world-wide*

Cf. also §§136-147.

§30. Adjectives can be divided into two categories from the point of view of stress:

(*a*) Those in which the accent in all other forms is on the same syllable as in the long form, e.g. **краси́вый — краси́в, краси́ва, краси́во, краси́вы — краси́вее**.

(*b*) Those in which the accent moves on to some other syllable in some parts of the short form and comparative, e.g. **крáсный — крáсен, краснá, крáсно, крáсны — красне́е**.

§31. Category (*a*): **Adjectives of three or more syllables in the nominative singular masculine have the accent fixed throughout all forms on the same syllable** (i.e. morpheme); (except for a few with mobile accent; see §§35, 37-40), e.g. **опáсный — опáсен, опáсна, опáсно, опáсны — опáснее** *dangerous*.

Similarly **богáтый** *rich*, **готóвый** *ready*, **кори́чневый** *brown*, **мéдленный** *slow*, **и́скренний** *sincere* (short form: **и́скренен, и́скренна, и́скренне** or **и́скренно, и́скренни** or **и́скренны**), etc.

This category includes all adjectives derived by means of suffixes from nouns, verbs or other adjectives, e.g.

несча́стный	*unhappy*	уве́ренный	*certain*
обы́чный	*usual*	замеча́тельный	*remarkable*
ра́достный	*joyful*	удиви́тельный	*surprising*
свобо́дный	*free*	необходи́мый	*necessary*
очередно́й	*recurrent, next*	краси́вый	*beautiful*
совреме́нный	*contemporary*	прекра́сный	*beautiful*
худо́жественный	*artistic*	желтова́тый	*yellowish*
поня́тный	*understandable*	хоро́шенький	*pretty*
похо́жий	*similar, like*		

In a few adjectives the stress within the stem may vary—note for instance the short form of **счастли́вый** *happy*, which may have the accent either on the suffix like the long form, or on the stem: **счастли́в, счастли́ва**, etc., or **сча́стлив, сча́стлива**, etc.

This category also includes most adjectives with foreign roots, e.g. **интере́сный** *interesting*, **серьёзный** *serious*, **комфорта́бельный** *comfortable*.

§32. Relative adjectives, being derived from nouns or other parts of speech, also come into this category, but of course do not have short forms or comparative, e.g.

Бо́жий	*God's*	деревя́нный	*wooden*
рабо́чий	*working*	желе́зный	*iron*
вое́нный	*military*	де́тский	*children's*
ли́чный	*personal*	мужско́й	*man's, male*
ночно́й	*nocturnal*	же́нский	*woman's, female*
ра́зный	*various*	ру́сский	*Russian*

Adjectives in **-ский** never have short forms (except a few in which -ский is not an added suffix, e.g. **пло́ский**, §37). Similarly all adjectives with soft **-н-** ending have no short forms, e.g.

вну́тренний	*internal*	после́дний	*last*
дома́шний	*domestic*	сре́дний	*middle*

синь is not used

except **си́ний** *blue*, **и́скренний** *sincere* (see §§37 and 31 respectively), and **дре́вний** *ancient*, which has fixed stress in short forms (but note comparative, §42).

§33. A few common adjectives of two syllables also have fixed stress. Such are:

ве́чный (ве́чен, ве́чна)	*eternal*
дре́вний (дре́вен, дре́вня)	*ancient*
ле́стный (ле́стен, ле́стна)	*flattering*
ло́жный (ло́жен, ло́жна)	*false*

смéртный (смéртен, смéртна)	*mortal*
чýдный (чýден, чýдна)	*wonderful*
чуднóй (чудён, чуднá)	*strange, odd*
я́вный (я́вен, я́вна)	*evident*
рад (no long form)	*glad*

§34. Category (*b*): **Nearly all common basic adjectives** (not derived from other words, and mostly having only two syllables in the masculine singular) **have mobile stress in the short form and comparative**. Such are дóбрый, крáсный, ýзкий and many others (see §37-43 below).

§35. The common adjectives of three syllables with mobile stress are: вели́кий *great*, весёлый *merry*, высóкий *high*, глубóкий *deep*, голóдный *hungry*, горя́чий *hot*, далёкий *distant*, дорогóй *dear*, жестóкий *cruel*, зелёный *green*, корóткий *short*, молодóй *young*, тяжёлый *heavy*, холóдный *cold*, хорóший *good*, широ́кий *wide*. Cf. §§37-40.

SHORT FORM

§36. In all the common adjectives mentioned above in Category (*b*) (see §34) the accent moves on to the ending in the feminine short form at least, e.g.

    ти́хий — тих, тихá, ти́хо, ти́хи.

Four groups with different patterns follow, but, since in modern Russian the groups in §§38 and 39 present on the whole only 'permissible' alternative patterns, these could be ignored for practical purposes and groups one to three (§§37-39) taken together under a rough general rule that **for the majority of basic adjectives the accent remains on the stem in the short form except for the feminine, where it moves on to the ending**. The obligatory exceptions to this 'rule' would then be only those listed under §33 above and §40 below. Note however that adjectives in the categories described in §32 as well as the isolated cases большóй and мáленький do not have short forms.

§37. The largest group consists of adjectives in which **the accent moves on to the ending in the feminine short form only**, e.g.

    прáвый — прав, правá, прáво, прáвы.

Note that this is the most common pattern even for adjectives with stress on the endings in the long form, e.g.

    прямóй — прям, прямá, пря́мо, пря́мы.

In some three-syllable adjectives the accent in masculine, neuter and plural short forms moves *back* one or more syllables from its position in the long form, e.g.

весёлый — ве́сел, весела́, ве́село, ве́селы.

Similarly дешёвый, дорого́й, зелёный, молодо́й.

Adjectives with this pattern include:

бы́стрый	quick	ско́рый	swift
весёлый (ве́сел, весела́)	merry	скро́мный (скро́мен)	modest
гла́дкий (гла́док)	smooth	сла́вный (сла́вен)	glorious
глу́пый	stupid	сла́дкий (сла́док)	sweet
го́лый	naked	сло́жный (сло́жен)	complicated
го́рький (го́рек)	bitter	сме́лый	bold
гро́мкий (гро́мок)	loud	стра́нный (стра́нен)	strange
гру́бый	coarse	стра́стный (стра́стен)	passionate
дешёвый (дёшев)	cheap		
ди́кий	wild	стро́гий	strict
до́лгий (до́лог)	long	тве́рдый (твёрд, тверда́)	firm, hard
жа́лкий (жа́лок)	pitiful	ти́хий	quiet
жа́ркий (жа́рок)	hot	то́нкий (то́нок)	thin
жесто́кий	cruel	це́лый	whole
жи́дкий (жи́док)	thin (liquid)	ча́стый	frequent
зелёный (зе́лен)	green	че́стный (че́стен)	honest
кра́сный (кра́сен)	red	чу́ждый (чужд)	alien
кре́пкий (кре́пок)	strong	я́ркий (я́рок)	bright
кру́глый (кругл)	round		
кру́пный (кру́пен)	big	глухо́й	deaf
ме́лкий (ме́лок)	small	дорого́й (до́рог)	dear
мо́дный (мо́ден)	fashionable	живо́й	alive
мо́крый (мокр)	wet	круто́й	steep
мя́гкий (мя́гок)	soft	молодо́й (мо́лод)	young
о́бщий (общ)	general	немо́й	dumb
о́стрый (остр)	sharp (see below)	плохо́й	bad
пло́ский (пло́сок)	flat	прямо́й	straight
пра́вый	right	пусто́й	empty
пья́ный	drunk	свято́й	holy
ре́дкий (ре́док)	rare	седо́й	grey
ре́зкий (ре́зок)	sharp, harsh	слепо́й	blind
ро́вный (ро́вен)	flat, even	сухо́й	dry
све́тлый (све́тел)	light (see below)	тупо́й	blunt
се́рый	grey	худо́й	bad
си́ний (синь, синя́)	dark blue		

(margin note: Дорога́ *)*

(margin note: pl. плóх... *)*

As a predicate the neuter form of **све́тлый** is **светло́**, e.g. **уже́ светло́** *it's already light.*

In the sense *witty* **о́стрый** has short forms **остёр, остра́, остро́,** ‖ **остры́.**

Note the exceptional accentuation of **ро́вный** in the phrase **неровён час** *you never know* (*anything might happen*).

Compounds of these adjectives have fixed stress, e.g. **модна́** but **старомо́дна** *old-fashioned,* **славна́** but **правосла́вна** *orthodox,* **страстна́** *passionate* but **бесстра́стна** *passionless* (cf. §41 below).

§38. Many other adjectives have the ending of the feminine short form stressed, but have an **alternative for the plural,** which may have the ending stressed or unstressed, e.g.

         ви́дный — ви́ден, видна́, ви́дно, ви́дны or **видны́.**

(The tendency to stress the ending of the plural short form is growing ‖ in modern Russian.)

Adjectives with this pattern include:

бе́дный (бе́ден)	poor	но́вый	new
бле́дный (бле́ден)	pale	ну́жный (ну́жен)	necessary
бли́зкий (бли́зок)	near	си́льный (си́лен or	
бо́дрый (бодр)	cheerful	силён)	strong
ва́жный (ва́жен)	important	ску́чный (ску́чен)	dull
ве́рный (ве́рен)	true	сла́бый	weak
ви́дный (ви́ден)	visible	слы́шный (слы́шен)	audible
вку́сный (вку́сен)	tasty	стра́шный (стра́-	
вре́дный (вре́ден)	harmful	шен)	terrible
голо́дный (го́ло-		те́сный (те́сен)	cramped
ден)	hungry	то́лстый	thick, fat
го́рдый	proud	тру́дный (тру́ден)	difficult
гру́стный (грус-		у́зкий (у́зок)	narrow
тен)	sad	холо́дный (хо́лоден)	cold
гря́зный (гря́зен)	dirty	чи́стый	clean
до́брый (добр)	good	я́сный (я́сен)	clear
дру́жный (дру́жен)	friendly		
ми́лый	nice	густо́й	thick, dense
не́жный (не́жен)	tender	дурно́й (ду́рен)	bad
ни́зкий (ни́зок)	low	просто́й	simple

Больно́й *ill* always has the ending stressed in the plural short form: **бо́лен, больна́, бо́льно** (adv.), **больны́.**

The normal adverb from **до́брый** is **добро́** *well,* but in some phrases the ending is stressed: **Добро́ бы сам сде́лал, а то всё** переложи́л на други́х *It wouldn't have been so bad if he had done it himself, but he foisted it on to the others*; Добро́ пожа́ловать! *Welcome!*

Compounds of these adjectives have fixed stress, e.g. верна́ but суеве́рна *superstitious*; вкусна́ but безвку́сна *tasteless*; видна́ but очеви́дна *obvious*; трудна́ but многотру́дна *laborious* (cf. §41).

§39. A further group of adjectives has the ending of the feminine short form stressed and that of **both the neuter and the plural stressed or not**, either being permissible, e.g.

> высо́кий — высо́к, высока́, высо́ко or высоко́, высо́ки or высоки́.

Adjectives with this pattern include:

бе́лый	*white*	мёртвый (мёртв)	*dead*
вели́кий	*great*	по́лный (по́лон)	*full*
высо́кий	*high*	ста́рый	*old*
глубо́кий	*deep*	тёмный (тёмен)	*dark*
далёкий	*distant*	тёплый (тёпел)	*warm*
дли́нный (дли́нен)	*long*	у́мный (умён)	*clever*
жёлтый	*yellow*	чёрный (чёрен)	*black*
коро́ткий (коро́-ток)	*short*	широ́кий	*wide*

Коро́ткий has the alternatives: ко́роток/коро́ток, коротка́, ко́ротко/коро́тко/коротко́, ко́ротки/коро́тки/коротки́.

Sometimes there is a difference in usage between the two patterns, e.g. вели́кий has, in the sense (*too*) *big* — вели́к, велика́, велико́, велики́; but in the sense *great* it has вели́к, велика́, вели́ко, вели́ки. Similarly for literally *dead* мёртво, мёртвы are used, but in a figurative sense мертво́, мертвы́ are used, e.g. лю́ди бы́ли мёртвы *the people were dead*, леса́ бы́ли мертвы́ *the forests were dead still*.

With a few adjectives of dimension, notably дли́нный and коро́ткий, there is a tendency to use the form with stress on the ending to denote an excess of the quality, e.g. пальто́ ему́ коротко́ *the coat is too short for him*, рукава́ длинны́ *the sleeves are too long*, as compared with сообще́ние ко́ротко *the announcement is short*, ре́чи бы́ли дли́нны *the speeches were long*. Yet another form of коро́ткий occurs only in some fixed phrases from folklore, e.g. ум ко́роток *he hasn't much brain*, сча́стье ко́ротко *happiness is short-lived*.

Adverbs from these normally have the stress on the ending: далеко́. Three have free alternatives: высоко́ or высо́ко, глубоко́ or **глубо́ко, широко́** or **широ́ко**; but with some a less common (archaic or folklore) alternative exists: **далеко́** (or **дале́ко**), **темно́** (or **тёмно**), **тепло́** (or **тёпло**). Stress is on the stem in the adverb **по́лно** and normally in **ко́ротко** (e.g. **ко́ротко говоря́...** *briefly...*) but stress is on the stem in some fixed phrases, e.g. (in folklore) **до́лго ли, коро́тко ли...** *how long it took I don't know*.

Compounds of **у́мный** have fixed stress, e.g. **умён, умна́, у́мно/умно́, у́мны/умны́** but **остроу́мный — остроу́мен, остроу́мна, остроу́мно, остроу́мны** *witty*; similarly **разу́мный** *reasonable* (cf. §41).

§40. Some adjectives have the **accent on the endings throughout the short form**, e.g.

      хоро́ший — хоро́ш, хороша́, хорошо́, хороши́.

до́лжен, должна́	*must*	**ра́вный (ра́вен)**	*equal*
горя́чий	*hot*	**све́жий**	*fresh*
лёгкий (лёгок)	*light, easy*	**смешно́й(смешо́н)**	*funny*
ма́лый	*small*	**тяжёлый**	*heavy*
о́стрый (остёр)	*witty*(cf.§37)	**хоро́ший**	*good*

and the pronouns **како́в?** *what (is it) like?* and **тако́в** *such, that kind of*.

A few of these have an alternative plural form with unstressed ending, e.g. **лёгкий — лёгок, легка́, легко́, легки́** or **лёгки**. Similarly **све́жий**.

Note that **здоро́вый**, being of three syllables, has fixed stress in the short form (but not comparative!) in the normal sense of *healthy, well*; but in the *colloquial* sense *strong* it has the accent on the endings: **здоро́в, здорова́, здорово́, здоровы́**. The adverb *very much* is **здо́рово**, but in other senses the adverb, like the colloquial greeting *hullo* is stressed **здоро́во**.

§41. Basic adjectives as the second element in compound adjectives usually lose their mobile stress (the compounds thus conforming to the general rule in §31 above about derived adjectives) e.g. **красна́** *red* — **прекра́сна** *beautiful*; **модна́** *fashionable* — **старомо́дна** *old-fashioned*; **умна́** *intelligent* — **остроу́мна** *witty*, etc. (cf. §§37, 38, 39).

Adjectives made negative by the prefix **без-** lose their mobile stress, e.g. **вкусна́** *tasty* — **безвку́сна** *tasteless*; **шумна́** *noisy* — **бесшу́мна** *noiseless*, but those with **не-** prefixed generally retain their original stress pattern, e.g. **глуп, глупа́, глу́по — неглу́п, неглупа́, неглу́по; хоро́ш, хороша́, хорошо́, хороши́ — нехоро́ш, нехороша́, нехорошо́, нехороши́**.

With the prefix **полу-, живо́й** *alive* and **мёртвый** *dead* retain their original stress, e.g. **полужива́, полужи́вы** *half dead*.

COMPARATIVE

§42. (*a*) **All comparatives formed regularly by adding the suffix -ee or -ей have the stress on the same syllable as in the feminine short form.** Thus, in fact, most common disyllabic adjectives have the ending of the comparative stressed, while most longer adjectives retain the accent on the stem in the comparative, e.g.

кра́сный — красна́ — красне́е	*redder*
бе́дный — бедна́ — бедне́е	*poorer*
дли́нный — длинна́ — длинне́е	*longer*
прямо́й — пряма́ — пряме́е	*straighter*
	etc.

but

краси́вый — краси́ва — краси́вее	*more beautiful*
свобо́дный — свобо́дна — свобо́днее	*more free*
серьёзный — серьёзна — серьёзнее	*more serious*
	etc.

Дре́вний, with stress on the stem in short forms, has comparative древне́е.

The following common trisyllabic adjectives have stress on the ending of the comparative: весёлый — веселе́е; голо́дный — голодне́е; здоро́вый — здорове́е; зелёный — зелене́е; тяжёлый — тяжеле́е; холо́дный — холодне́е; горя́чий — горяче́е. (Cf. stress in short forms, §§37, 38, 40.)

(*b*) Many common basic adjectives, however, have special forms in the comparative, with the consonant of the stem modified (and sometimes the stem shortened), stress on the stem, and the ending **-e**. Most of these have stems ending in к, г, х, т or д. Note particularly those with endings stressed in the long form, which move the accent on to the stem in this form:

большо́й — бо́льше and бо́лее	молодо́й — моло́же
глухо́й — глу́ше	плохо́й — пло́ше (little used)
густо́й — гу́ще	просто́й — про́ще
дорого́й — доро́же	сухо́й — су́ше
круто́й — кру́че	худо́й — ху́же

бли́зкий — бли́же	гро́мкий — гро́мче
бога́тый — бога́че	далёкий — да́льше or да́лее
высо́кий — вы́ше	дешёвый — деше́вле
гла́дкий — гла́же	до́лгий — до́льше
глубо́кий — глу́бже	жа́лкий — жа́льче
го́рький — го́рче	жа́ркий — жа́рче

(depending on the meaning)

жёсткий — жёстче	сла́дкий — сла́ще
жи́дкий — жи́же	ста́рый — ста́рше or старе́е
коро́ткий — коро́че	стро́гий — стро́же
кре́пкий — кре́пче	твёрдый — твёрже
лёгкий — ле́гче	ти́хий — ти́ше
ма́лый — ме́ньше or ме́нее	то́лстый — то́лще
ме́лкий — ме́льче	то́нкий — то́ньше
мя́гкий — мя́гче	у́зкий — у́же
ни́зкий — ни́же	ча́стый — ча́ще
по́здний — по́зже or поздне́е	чи́стый — чи́ще
ра́нний — ра́ньше or ра́нее	широ́кий — ши́ре
ре́дкий — ре́же	я́ркий — я́рче
ре́зкий — ре́зче	

A few common adjectives do not form simple comparatives, e.g. вели́кий, жесто́кий and usually ди́кий.

§43. Note the contrast in stress between **большо́й** *big* and **бо́льший** *bigger, greater*. In oblique cases the position of stress is sometimes clear from the spelling, e.g. **по большо́й ме́ре** *in great measure*, **по бо́льшей ме́ре** *in greater measure*; **в большо́м масшта́бе** *on a big scale*, **в бо́льшем масшта́бе** *on a bigger scale*. Here stress on the ending is shown by writing the vowel **o**, an unstressed ending by writing **e** (cf. §3 above).

In many cases, however, the spelling of the two words is the same, and here it is customary to print an accent on the stem of **бо́льший** if there is any possibility of ambiguity, e.g. **с больши́м удовольст-вием** *with great pleasure* (stress on -ши́м) but **с бо́льшим удоволь-ствием** *with greater pleasure*.

Superlative

§44. The superlative suffix, where used, always bears the accent in basic shorter adjectives, and is unstressed in adjectives of three or more syllables (except most of the small number with mobile accent in the basic form), e.g. **крупне́йший** *biggest*, **бедне́йший** *poorest*, **нижа́йший** *lowest*, **глубоча́йший** *deepest*; but **холо́днейший** *coldest*, **интере́снейший** *most interesting*, **серьёзнейший** *most serious*.

Chapter 4

PRONOUNS

§45. In the possessive pronouns **мой** *my*, **твой** *your*, **свой** *one's*, stress is on the endings in all cases, e.g.

мой, моя, моё; мой — моего, моему, моей; мойх, мойм, мойми

Note that in these pronouns, as in **сам** *oneself*, the accent in the gen. and dat.sing. masculine and neuter falls on the final syllable as in the pronouns **его, ему**, and not as in stressed endings of adjectives, e.g. **большого, большому**. But note the departure from this in the phrases with **по** meaning *in my/your opinion* or *way*: **по-моему, по-твоему**; *in one's own way*: **по-своему**. In these stress is on the stem of the pronoun. (If the noun *opinion* is expressed, however, the stress is normal: **по моему мнению**.)

§46. The difference in stress between **сам, сама, само**; pl. **сами** *oneself* with stress on the endings, and **самый, самая, самое; самые** *the very, the most* with stress fixed on the stem, is not apparent from the spelling in most cases, e.g.

Я видел его самого.	*It was* him (*himself*) *I saw.*
Я видел его у самого берега.	*I saw him right at the shore (at the very shore).*
Письмо написано самой Павловой.	*The letter was written by Pavlova herself.*
Сочинение написано той самой студенткой.	*The essay was written by that very student.*

But note the vowel in endings with **и** or **ы**:

Это было сказано самим Пушкиным.	*This was said by Pushkin himself.*
Это было сказано тем самым человеком.	*This was said by that very person.*

§47. Note the contrast in stress between the negative pronouns and adverbs **никто, никого** *nobody*; **ничто, ничего** *nothing*; **никогда** *never*; **нигде, никуда** *nowhere*; etc., and those with **не-** (which represent **нет** plus **кого, нет** plus **где**, etc.), e.g. **некого** *there is nobody*; **нечего** *there is nothing*; **некогда** *there is no time*; **негде отдохнуть** *there is nowhere to rest*; **некуда идти** *there is nowhere to go*, etc. In these the **не-** remains the stressed element even when the phrase is broken up by a preposition, e.g. **не с кем говорить** *there is no-one to talk to*; **не за что** *don't mention it* (*there is nothing for which to*

thank me). Contrast **Я не говори́л ни с ке́м** *I spoke to no-one;*
ни за что́ *not for anything.*

The accent is on **не-** also in the indefinite pronouns and adverbs
не́кто *someone;* **не́что** *something;* **не́который** *some;* **не́сколько**
several; **не́когда** *once, at one time;* etc. but not in **немно́го** *some,*
which is a normally negated pronoun (cf. adjectives like **некраси́вый**).

§48. The indefinite suffixes **-то, -либо** and **-нибудь** are always unstressed and pronounced as one unit with the pronoun or adverb,
e.g. **кто́-то** *someone* (pronounced [ˈktɔtə]); **что́-либо** *anything;* **где́-**
нибудь *anywhere,* etc.

The prefix **кое-** has secondary stress, e.g. **ко̀е-кто́** *somebody;* **ко̀е-**
что́ *something.*

§49. In printed texts (unstressed) the pronoun *what* is sometimes
distinguished from the conjunction *that* by an accent, e.g.

Я зна́ю, что он бу́дет петь.   *I know (that) he will sing.*
Я зна́ю, что́ он бу́дет петь.   *I know what he will sing.*

For stress of pronouns in connected speech see further §§101, 102.

CHAPTER 5

NUMERALS

§50. In many numerals, the accent moves on to the endings in all oblique cases, e.g.

(*a*) Those with endings like pronouns: **оди́н, одна́** . . . **одного́, одному́** . . . **одно́й**; pl. **одни́, одни́х, одни́м** *one*. Similarly the collective numerals **дво́е, двои́х** *two*; **тро́е, трои́х** *three*. Stress is fixed on the stem, however, in **о́ба, о́бе** *both*: **обо́их, обо́им; обе́их, обе́им.**

(*b*) **Два, двух, двумя́** *two*. Similarly **три, трёх, тремя́** *three*; **четы́ре, четырёх, четырьмя́** *four*.

(*c*) The numbers from five to ten, twenty and thirty have the form of feminine nouns ending in **-ь**, with stress on the endings, e.g. **пять, пяти́, пятью́** *five*; **во́семь, восьми́, восьмью́** *eight*; **де́сять, десяти́, десятью́** *ten*; **два́дцать, двадцати́, двадцатью́** *twenty*. (But in carrying out *multiplication* stress in these numerals remains on the stem, e.g. **пя́тью пять — 25**, *five times five are twenty five*; **во́семью во́семь — 64**, *eight eights are sixty four*.)

(*d*) Compound numerals. The other multiples of ten from fifty to eighty decline in both parts, but have only one stressed syllable, e.g.

пятьдеся́т, пяти́десяти, пятью́десятью	*fifty*
се́мьдесять, семи́десяти, семью́десятью	*seventy*

Similarly the hundreds, e.g.

пятьсо́т, пятисо́т, пятьюста́ми	*five hundred*
девятьсо́т, девятисо́т, девятьюста́ми	*nine hundred*

Except 200 and 300, which have secondary stress on the instrumental case ending, and 400, which has this also in the genitive/prepositional:

две́сти, двухсо́т, двумяста́ми
четы́реста, четырёхсо́т, четырьмяста́ми.

(*e*) **со́рок** *forty* has **сорока́** for all oblique cases.

§51. In **треть** *a third* and **че́тверть** *a quarter* the accent is on the stem in the singular and the nominative plural, but moves on to the endings in the other cases in the plural:

че́тверть, че́тверти — че́тверти, четверте́й, четвертя́м, etc.

In **полови́на** *a half* accent is fixed. The prefix **пол-**, however, declines in **полтора́** (fem. **полторы́**) *one and a half* and **полтора́ста** *one hundred and fifty*, with the forms **полу́тора** and **полу́тораста** in all oblique cases. Similarly in **по́лдень** *midday* and **по́лночь** *midnight*, **пол-** may be declined (or not, the stress varying accordingly), e.g. **полу́дня, полу́дню**, etc. or **по́лдня, по́лдню**, etc.; **полу́ночи** or **по́лночи**. The other type of compound consisting of **пол-** and a noun in the genitive case, e.g. **полго́да** *half a year*, usually has fixed stress in oblique cases, e.g. gen. **полуго́да**, instr. **полуго́дом**; but in **полчаса́** *half an hour* the accent shifts: gen. **получа́са**, instr. **получа́сом**. (The frequently used prefix **полу-**, on the other hand, does not decline and is always unstressed, e.g. **полукру́г** *semicircle*.)

§52. The accent is fixed on the stem in:

(a) The numerals which are in fact three-syllable nouns, i.e. **полови́на** *half*, **ты́сяча** *thousand* (instr.sing. **ты́сячей** or **ты́сячью**; gen. pl. **ты́сяч**); **миллио́н** *million*.

(b) The teens. Note the stressed syllable: the first element in **оди́ннадцать** *eleven*, **четы́рнадцать** *fourteen*; but in all others **-на-**, e.g. **двена́дцать** *twelve*, **восемна́дцать** *eighteen*.

(c) **Девяно́сто** *ninety*, with **девяно́ста** in all oblique cases; **сто** *hundred* with **ста** in all oblique cases.

§53. The numerals **два/две, три, пять** to **де́сять, со́рок** and **сто** when following prepositions frequently become unstressed; see §106*a*.

§54. The ordinal numerals have fixed stress (and no short forms). Note the final stress in **шесто́й** *sixth*, **седьмо́й** *seventh*, **восьмо́й** *eighth*, and **сороково́й** *fortieth*.

CHAPTER 6

ADVERBS

§55. Sometimes the stress of a word used as an adverb differs from that of the normal form, e.g.

бего́м	*at a run*	from бег, бе́гом	*running*
верхо́м	*on horseback*	from верх, ве́рхом	*top*
круго́м	*round about*	from круг, кру́гом	*circle*
домо́й	*home(ward)*	from дом, до́ма	*house*
полны́м-полно́	*full up*	from по́лный, по́лным	*full*
(cf. давны́м-давно́ *long ago*)			
вполне́	*fully, completely*	from по́лный	
вообще́	*in general, at all*	from о́бщий	*general*
впервы́е	*for the first time*	from пе́рвый	*first*

A few gerunds in **-а** have different stress when used as adverbs, e.g.

молча́	*being silent*	but мо́лча	*silently*
стоя́	*while standing*	but сто́я	*upright*

§56. (*a*) Adverbs derived from the neuter short form of adjectives (including participles) as a rule have the same stress as the neuter short form, e.g. **я́рко** *brightly*; **хо́лодно** *coldly*; **хорошо́** *well*; **вызыва́юще** *defiantly*; but a few require special attention, e.g. **ко́ротко** *briefly*—see §39.

(*b*) Adverbs derived from adjectives ending in **-ский/-ско́й** and other suffixes (with or without the prefix **по-**) generally have the same stress as the adjective, e.g. **дру́жески** *in a friendly way*; **мастерски́** *in a masterly way*; **по-ру́сски** *in Russian*; **по-но́вому** *in a new way*; **по-ви́димому** *apparently*.

(*c*) Adverbs derived from preposition plus noun or preposition plus adjective have a variety of stress, for which no useful rules can be formulated, e.g.

добела́ *white-hot*; **догола́** *naked*; **докрасна́** or **до́красна** *red-hot*; **до́чиста** *till spotlessly clean*.
на́бело *clean (copy)*; **на́спех** *hurriedly*; **на́двое** *in two*; but **наве́рно(е)** *probably*; **напра́во** *on the right*; **намно́го** *by far*; **надо́лго** *for a long time*; **на́голо** *bare (shorn)* but **наголо́** *naked (of a sword)*. **по́просту** *simply*; **по́пусту** *to no purpose*; but **подо́лгу** *long, for ages*; **поско́льку** *so far as*.

и́здали *from a distance*; и́здавна *since long ago*; и́зредка *now and then*; but изнутри́ *from within*; издалека́ *from afar*.

задо́лго *long in advance*; заодно́ *all at once*; but за́муж(ем) *married*.

свысока́ *haughtily*; сгоряча́ *in the heat of the moment*; сперва́ *at first*; but сле́ва *on the left*; сно́ва *again*; снача́ла *at first*.

Note the stress of отча́сти *partly*; сейча́с *now*; то́тчас *immediately*; совсе́м *quite*; во́все не *not at all*. Cf. also §106.

§57. Note the stress in pairs or trios of adverbs of place (mainly derived from preposition plus noun in locative, accusative or genitive case) denoting position at rest, or movement, e.g.

Он пошёл наве́рх/вниз.	*He went upstairs/downstairs.*
Он живёт наверху́/внизу́.	*He lives upstairs/downstairs.*
Чита́я све́рху вниз.	*Reading from top to bottom.*
Он сде́лал шаг вперёд/ назад.	*He took a step forward/back.*
Впереди́ показа́лся лес.	*A wood appeared in front.*
Мы оста́вили лес позади́.	*We left the wood behind.*
Она́ огляде́ла себя́ сперва́ спе́реди, пото́м сза́ди.	*She looked at herself first from in front, then from behind.*

The pair of adverbs вдво́е and вдвоём show a similar distinction of accusative/locative case, e.g.

Оно́ вдво́е бо́льше.	*It is twice as big.*
Они́ живу́т вдвоём.	*They live together (the two of them).*

Similarly втро́е/втроём; вче́тверо/вчетверо́м, etc.

§58. Note the change in stress when certain basic adverbs have either a preposition or не- prefixed:

давно́	*long ago*	but неда́вно	*recently*
куда́	*where (to)*	but отку́да	*where from*
сюда́	*here*	but отсю́да	*from here*
туда́	*there*	but отту́да	*from there*

In the sense *there is not anywhere, there is no time*, etc., не- is stressed: не́где, не́куда, не́откуда, не́когда.

The normal negative adverbs *nowhere, never*, etc. with prefix ни- retain their original stress: нигде́, никуда́, ниотку́да, никогда́ (cf. §47).

CHAPTER 7

VERBS

§59. For our purpose verbs can be divided into two basic categories:

(*a*) Those with monosyllabic infinitive (including as 'monosyllabic' all infinitives in -ти and -чь, e.g. нести́, бере́чь).

(*b*) Those with two or more syllables in the infinitive (and a few regular monosyllabic verbs like знать).

§60. The accent is fixed on the same syllable (morpheme) **throughout all parts of all tenses and forms in verbs with the ending of the infinitive unstressed,** e.g.

де́лать — де́лаю, де́лает — де́лала — сде́ланный — де́лая
to do, make

ве́рить — ве́рю, ве́рит — ве́рила — (у)-ве́ренный — ве́ря
to believe

ви́деть — ви́жу, ви́дит — ви́дела — уви́денный — ви́дя *to see*
мёрзнуть — мёрзну, мёрзнет — мёрзла *to freeze*

§61. Stress is likely to be mobile in verbs with (*a*) monosyllabic infinitives; and (*b*) stress on the infinitive ending, e.g.

(*a*) звать — зову́, зовёт — звала́ — зва́нный/звана́ *to call*
нести́ — несу́, несёт — нёс, несла́ — несённый/несена́
to carry

(*b*) писа́ть — пишу́, пи́шет — писа́ла — пи́санный/пи́сана
to write

купи́ть — куплю́, ку́пит — купи́ла — ку́пленный/ку́плена
to buy

тяну́ть — тяну́, тя́нет — тяну́ла — тя́нутый *to pull*
коло́ть — колю́, ко́лет — коло́ла — ко́лотый *to chop, split*

Mobility affects particularly the Present/future tense, the Past tense, and the Past participle passive, the following general rules applying unless otherwise stated:

§62. Present/future tense

(*a*) The accent is fixed on the same syllable throughout in all Present/future tenses with the stem ending in a vowel, e.g.

чита́ю, чита́ет; уме́ю, уме́ет; стою́, стои́т; стро́ю, стро́ит.

(*b*) In all conjugations, if the accent falls on the stem in the first person singular of the Pres./fut., it will be fixed on the stem throughout the tense, e.g.

зна́ю, зна́ет; мо́ю, мо́ет; пла́чу, пла́чет; ви́жу, ви́дит; слы́шу, слы́шит;

whereas, if the accent is on the ending of the 1st sing., it may or may not remain there in other parts of the tense, e.g.

говорю́, говори́шь   but   хожу́, хо́дишь.

(*c*) The stress of the Present/future is mobile (falling on the ending in the first person sing. but on the stem throughout the rest of the tense) in:

(i) many verbs of the second conjugation having the accent on the ending in the Infinitive, e.g.

ходи́ть — хожу́, хо́дит   *to go*
смотре́ть — смотрю́, смо́трит   *to look*
держа́ть — держу́, де́ржит   *to hold*

(but not all verbs with such infinitives have mobile stress). Cf. §§75*a*, 77*b*, 81, 85*b*, 92.

(ii) verbs of the first conjugation with accent on the Infinitive ending -**ать** and consonant change in the Present/future, e.g. писа́ть — пишу́, пи́шет *to write*. Cf. §72*b*.

(iii) all verbs in -**оть**, e.g. боро́ться—борю́сь, бо́рется *to struggle*. Cf. §82.

(iv) a few verbs in -**нуть**, e.g. тяну́ть—тяну́, тя́нет *to pull*. Cf. §81.

(v) some verbs with the monosyllabic root *-**ять**, e.g. приня́ть — приму́, при́мет *to take*. Cf. §92.

(*d*) The endings of the first conjugation have the accent falling on them (and therefore the **е** modified to **ё**) in:

(i) most verbs with monosyllabic infinitives, e.g. нести́ — несу́, несёт *to carry*. Cf. §91 for exceptions.

(ii) most verbs in -**нуть** with stress on the ending of the infinitive, e.g. верну́ть — верну́, вернёт (pfv.) *to return*. Cf. §§80-81.

(iii) verbs ending in -**овать**/-**евать** in which -**овать** is not an added suffix, e.g. жева́ть — жую́, жуёт *to chew*. Cf. §73*c*.

(iv) умере́ть (pfv.) *to die*, тере́ть *to wipe*, *rub* and other compounds of these, and compounds of -**переть**, e.g. запере́ть *to lock*: умру́, умрёт, etc. Cf. §76*c*.

(v) a few verbs in -**ать**, including all in -**авать**, e.g. дава́ть—даю́, даёт *to give*, встава́ть — встаю́, встаёт *to stand up*, смея́ться — смеюсь, смеётся *to laugh*. Cf. §74.

§63. Imperative, and Gerund in -я/-а

The stress of the Imperative and Gerund in **-я/-а** is generally like that of the first sing. of the Present/future tense, e.g.

**смотре́ть — смотрю́, смо́трит — смотри́ — смотря́
чита́ть — чита́ю, чита́ет — чита́й — чита́я.**

But cf. §55.

§64. Present participle active

The stress of the Present participle active is generally like that of the 3rd person singular (or plural) of the Present tense, e.g.

**чита́ет — чита́ющий   пи́шет — пи́шущий
говори́т — говоря́щий**

except in verbs of the second conjugation with mobile stress in the Present tense, e.g. **хо́дит** but **ходя́щий**; **де́ржит** but **держа́щий**. Cf. §§75*a*, 77*b*(ii), 85*b*.

§65. Present participle passive

The stress of the Present participle passive depends on the conjugation:

For verbs of the first conjugation it has the stress of the first person plural, e.g. **де́лать — де́лаем — де́лаемый**; **чита́ть — чита́ем — чита́емый**; **угова́ривать — угова́риваем — угова́риваемый**; **тре́бовать — тре́буем — тре́буемый**; **организова́ть — организу́ем — организу́емый**; **нести́ — несём — несо́мый**.

For verbs of the second conjugation it has the stress of the infinitive, e.g. **ви́деть — ви́дим — ви́димый**; **лови́ть — ло́вим — лови́мый**; **проси́ть — про́сим — проси́мый**; **слы́шать — слы́шим — слы́шимый**.

This participle is scarcely used in spoken Russian, and is lacking in many verbs.

Many words with this form have become fixed as adjectives, in this case frequently differing in stress from the basic verb (which is often a *perfective*), e.g. **не коле́блемый** *not being shaken*, but **непоколеби́мый** *unshakable, steadfast*; **спо́рить** *to argue* but **неоспори́мый** *incontestable*. Cf. §125*c*.

§66. Past tense, Past participle active and Gerund in -в

The stress of the Past tense, Past participle active and Gerund in **-в/-вши** is like that of the Infinitive, e.g.

писа́ть — писа́л, писа́ла — писа́вший — написа́в(ши).

The accent of the Past tense is mobile only in verbs with monosyllabic infinitive, e.g. **взял, взяла́, взя́ло, взя́ли**; **нёс, несла́, несло́, несли́** (cf. §93, 96) and a few verbs like **умере́ть** (cf. §76*c*) and **роди́ться** (see §85*a*).

§67. Past participle passive

(*a*) The stress of the Past participle passive in verbs of both conjugations is usually on the syllable before the infinitive suffix (i.e. remains fixed in infinitives with accent on the stem, and moves back a syllable in infinitives with accent on the ending), e.g.

де́лать — сде́ланный	образова́ть — образо́ванный
стро́ить — стро́енный	получи́ть — полу́ченный
чита́ть — чи́танный	тяну́ть — тя́нутый

(*b*) The suffix of the Past participle passive in **-енный** is, however, stressed (**-ённый**), in verbs with monosyllabic infinitives and in second conjugation verbs with the accent on the ending in the infinitive and throughout the Present tense (see §§97, 85), e.g. **нести́ — несённый; говори́ть — говорённый**.

(*c*) In the short form of the Past participle passive accent is mobile only in verbs with monosyllabic infinitives and in second conjugation verbs with the suffix of the participle stressed (**-ённый**) (see (*b*) above). Also in compounds of **пере́ть** (§76*c*). e.g.

звать — зван, звана́, зва́но, зва́ны

принести́ — принесён, принесена́, принесено́, принесены́

реши́ть — решён, решена́, решено́, решены́.

§68. Prefix вы-

In spite of anything said above, all *perfective* verbs of any conjugation with prefix **вы-** have the stress fixed on this prefix throughout all forms, e.g.

вы́йти — вы́йду, вы́йдет — вы́шел, вы́шла *to come/go out*

(Cf. for instance *to pass*: **пройти́ — пройду́, пройдёт — прошёл, прошла́.**)

Other examples are: **вы́брать** *to choose* — **вы́беру, вы́берет — вы́брал, вы́брала** (cf. *to take*: **брать—беру́, берёт—брал, брала́**); **вы́пить** *to drink* — **вы́пью, вы́пьет — вы́пил, вы́пила** (cf. imperfective: **пить — пью, пьёт — пил, пила́**); **вы́расти** *to grow* — **вы́расту, вы́растет — вы́рос, вы́росла** (cf. imperfective: **расти́ — расту́, растёт — рос, росла́**); **вы́ступить** *to come forward, perform* — **вы́ступлю, вы́ступит — вы́ступил** (cf. for instance *to enter*: **поступи́ть — поступлю́, посту́пит — поступи́л**).

Imperfectives with **вы-**, of course, retain their original stress, e.g. *to come/go out*: **выходи́ть — выхожу́, выхо́дит — выходи́л.**

For nouns with prefix **вы-** see §11.

§69. A more detailed treatment follows, the verbs being considered according to their Infinitives: those in **-ать, -еть, -уть, -оть** and **-ить** (§§70-87), and monosyllabic infinitives (including those in **-ти**) (§§88-100).

INFINITIVE IN -ать

§70. Irrespective of conjugation, the general rule in §60 above applies: if the accent is on the stem in the infinitive it is fixed on the stem throughout all parts, e.g.

де́лать — де́лаю, де́лает — де́лал — сде́ланный — де́лая
    to do, make

ре́зать — ре́жу, ре́жет — ре́зал — ре́занный — ре́жа *to cut*

слы́шать — слы́шу, слы́шит — слы́шал — слы́шанный —
    слы́ша *to hear.*

Note that all imperfective verbs with the frequentative suffix **-ывать/-ивать** have the accent on the stem in the Infinitive and therefore fixed throughout. In such verbs the accent has usually moved back from its position in the basic verb from which the 'new' imperfective has been derived, frequently with the characteristic change of an **o** in the stem to **a**, e.g.

говори́ть — разгова́ривать; рабо́тать — разраба́тывать.

A few examples are:

разраба́тывать	*to process*	**разгова́ривать**	*to converse*
опи́сывать	*to describe*	**расска́зывать**	*to tell*
осма́тривать	*to survey*	**спра́шивать**	*to ask*
остана́вливать	*to stop*	**устра́ивать**	*to arrange*

(This does not include, of course, finally-stressed infinitives ending in **-ывать/-ивать** in which **-ыв/-ив** is actually part of the stem of the verb, e.g. **забыва́ть** *to forget*, **открыва́ть** *to open*, **называ́ть** *to call*, **убива́ть** *to kill*, **налива́ть** *to pour*, etc.).

Verbs with the suffix **-ничать** always have the accent fixed on the stem, e.g. **у́мничать** *to show off one's intelligence*, **скро́мничать** *to adopt an air of modesty*, **спле́тничать** *to gossip, talk scandal.*

§71. Regular first conjugation:

(*a*) By far the greater number of regular first conjugation verbs with infinitive suffix **-ать/-ять** have the accent falling on the suffix in the Infinitive and fixed on it throughout, except that the Past participle passive suffix **-анный** (where it exists) scarcely ever bears the stress, which moves back one syllable on to the stem in this form only, e.g.

чита́ть — чита́ет — чита́л — (про)чи́танный *to read.*

Only a few examples of this very numerous class are given here:

игра́ть (сы́гранный)	*to play*
знать (у́знанный)	*to know*
лома́ть (сло́манный)	*to break*
меша́ть (сме́шанный *mixed*)	*to hinder; to stir*
обеща́ть (обе́щанный)	*to promise*
ожида́ть (неожи́данный *unexpected*)	*to expect*
пойма́ть (по́йманный) (pfv.)	*to catch*
теря́ть (поте́рянный)	*to lose*

Stress on the suffix **-анный** occurs only with monosyllabic verbs like **звать — зва́нный** and in the verb **жела́ть** *to wish* — **жела́нный**.

Many verbs with this type of Infinitive do not have a participle in **-анный**, either because they are intransitive or because they are imperfectives not adding a prefix to form the perfective, e.g. **помога́ть** *to help*, **пуска́ть** *release, allow*, **замеча́ть** *to remark, notice*, **возвраща́ть** *to return*, etc.

(*b*) Common simple verbs (i.e. not formed by adding prefixes or suffixes other than the suffix **-ать**) of regular first conjugation with stress on the stem throughout are:

бе́гать	*to run*	па́чкать	*to soil, stain*
ве́шать	*to hang* (trans.)	печа́тать	*to print*
де́лать	*to do, make*	пла́вать	*to swim, float*
дви́гать	*to move* (see	по́лзать	*to crawl*
(дви́гает)	also §72a)	пры́гать	*to jump*
дёргать	*to tug*	пу́тать	*to tangle,*
ду́мать	*to think*		*confuse*
за́втракать	*to breakfast*	рабо́тать	*to work*
ка́пать	*to drip* (see	слу́шать	*to listen*
	also §72a)	стря́пать	*to cook*
кла́няться	*to bow, greet*	сюсю́кать	*to lisp*
ку́шать	*to eat*	то́пать	*to stamp*
ме́шкать	*to delay, loiter*	у́жинать	*to have supper*
обе́дать	*to have dinner*	цара́пать	*to scratch*
па́дать	*to fall*	щу́пать	*to feel, touch*

Most compounds of **бе́гать, дви́гать, па́дать, по́лзать** have stress on the suffix and are imperfective, e.g. **убега́ть** (pfv. **убежа́ть**) *run away*, **передвига́ть** (pfv. **передви́нуть**) *move, shift*, **напада́ть** (pfv. **напа́сть**) *attack*, **вползáть** (pfv. **вползти́**) *crawl in*. (Cf. generally such verbs as **приходи́ть/прийти́** for the formation of aspectual pairs from verbs of motion.)

Compounds of these with stress on the stem are perfective (and may be compared with such perfectives as **походи́ть** *walk for some time*, **сходи́ть** *go there and back in a short time*), e.g. **забéгать** *begin to run* (cf. impfv. **забегáть**, pfv. **забежáть** *run into a place*); **напáдать** (third person only) *fall and pile up*, e.g. **напáдало мнóго снéга** (cf. above impfv. **нападáть** *attack*).

Special cases of this are **плáвать** and **клáняться** which form most compounds with the stems **-плывáть** and **-клоня́ть** e.g. **приплывáть/приплы́ть** *arrive by water*, **наклоня́ть/наклони́ть** *bend down*. **Плáвать** itself forms some perfectives, e.g. **наплáвать** *cover a certain distance by water*.

Similarly **ты́кать** (**ты́чет**) *poke* (§72a) forms imperfective compounds on the regular first conjugation stem **-тыкáть** with perfectives in **-ткнуть**, e.g. **втыкáть/воткну́ть** *poke into*.

Into this group come also **надéяться** — **надéюсь, надéется** *to hope*; **сéять** — **сéю, сéет** *to sow*; **тáять** — **тáет** *to thaw*; **лáять** — **лáю, лáет** *to bark*.

§72. First conjugation with consonant of stem modified throughout the Present/future tense:

(*a*) Those with the stress on the stem in the Infinitive have fixed stress throughout, including the Gerund in **-a** (cf. §60), e.g. **рéзать** — **рéжу, рéжет** — **рéзал** — **рéзанный** — **рéжа** *to cut*. Similarly:

дви́гать (**дви́жу, дви́жет**; also **дви́гаю, дви́гает**)	*to move*
кáпать (**кáплет**)	*to drip* (see also §71a)
мáзать (**мáжу, мáжет**)	*to oil, smear*
плáкать (**плáчу, плáчет**)	*to weep*
пря́тать (**пря́чу, пря́чет**)	*to hide*
сы́пать (**сы́плю, сы́плет**)	*to strew*
ты́кать (**ты́чу, ты́чет**)	*to poke*
éхать (**éду, éдет**)	*to travel*

Note in this connection aspectual pairs in which only the stress differentiates the two infinitives (and past tenses), e.g.

врезáть/врéзать — Pres. **врезáет**; Fut. **врéжет** *to cut into*
засыпáть/засы́пать — Pres. **засыпáет**; Fut. **засы́плет** *to cover, bury, fill up*

(*b*) Those with the stress on the ending in the Infinitive have mobile stress in the Present/future tense (i.e. on the ending in the 1st sing.,

on the stem in other parts), and stress on the stem in the Past participle passive, e.g. писа́ть — пишу́, пи́шет — писа́л — пи́санный
to write.

Similarly:

бормота́ть (бормочу́, бормо́чет)	*to mutter, mumble*
вяза́ть (вяжу́, вя́жет — свя́занный)	*to tie, knit*
дрема́ть (дремлю́, дре́млет)	*to doze, slumber*
иска́ть (ищу́, и́щет — и́сканный)	*to look for*
показа́ть (покажу́, пока́жет — пока́занный)	*to show*
(and other compounds of -казать)	
клевета́ть (клевещу́, клеве́щет)	*to slander*
лиза́ть (лижу́, ли́жет)	*to lick*
маха́ть (машу́, ма́шет, also, colloquially маха́ю, маха́ет)	*to wave*
паха́ть (пашу́, па́шет)	*to plough*
плеска́ть (плещу́, пле́щет)	*to splash*
пляса́ть (пляшу́, пля́шет)	*to dance*
ропта́ть (ропщу́, ро́пщет)	*to murmur, grumble*
свиста́ть (свищу́, сви́щет; also свисте́ть — свищу́, свисти́т)	*to whistle*
скака́ть (скачу́, ска́чет)	*to gallop*
топта́ть (топчу́, то́пчет)	*to trample*
трепета́ть (трепещу́, трепе́щет)	*to tremble*
хлеста́ть (хлещу́, хле́щет)	*to lash*
хлопота́ть (хлопочу́, хлопо́чет)	*to bustle*
хохота́ть (хохочу́, хохо́чет)	*to laugh loudly*
чеса́ть (чешу́, че́шет)	*to scratch, comb*
шепта́ть (шепчу́, ше́пчет)	*to whisper*
щекота́ть (щекочу́, щеко́чет)	*to tickle*
щипа́ть (щиплю́, щи́плет)	*to pinch*

The gerund in **-a**, where it occurs, has the accent on the ending:
ища́, шепча́.

Стона́ть *to groan* may be included here — стону́ (or стона́ю),
сто́нет.

Exceptions among this class of verbs are колеба́ть *to shake* (reflexive: *to fluctuate, hesitate*) and колыха́ться *to sway* (without **-ся**
to cause to sway), which have the accent on the stem throughout the
Present tense: коле́блюсь, коле́блется, Past part. pass. коле́блен-
ный, Gerund коле́блясь; колы́шется, Gerund колы́шась. (For
the latter verb the forms колыха́юсь, колыха́ется, etc. are considered colloquial.)

§73. First conjugation verbs with the Infinitive ending in the suffix -овать/-евать, the -ов- changing to -у-, the -ев- to -ю- or -у- in the Present tense. (Remember that this does not include verbs in which the -ов-/-ев- is part of the stem itself, e.g. здоро́ваться — здоро́вается *to greet*; одева́ться—одева́ется *to dress*; зева́ть—зева́ет *to yawn*. There are also a few exceptions like подразумева́ть — подразумева́ет *to imply*; намерева́ться — намерева́ется *to intend*.)

(*a*) Those with the accent in the Infinitive falling on any syllable other than the -ать have it fixed on that syllable throughout, e.g.

тре́бовать — тре́бует — тре́бованный   *to demand*
синтези́ровать — синтези́рует — синтези́ро-
    ванный   *to synthesise*
социализи́ровать — социализи́рует — социа-
    лизи́рованный   *to socialise*

(Cf. §73*d*(i), (iii) and (iv).)

(*b*) Those with the accent falling on -ать in the Infinitive have the stress on the -у- throughout the Present tense, but moving back on to the -ов in the Past participle passive, e.g.

образова́ть — образу́ет — образо́ванный   *to form, educate*
группирова́ть — группиру́ет — группиро́-
    ванный   *to group*
организова́ть — организу́ет — организо́-
    ванный   *to organise*
воева́ть — воюю, воюет — (завоёванный)   *to wage war*
    (cf. §73*d* (i)-(iii)).   (*conquer*)

(*c*) There are a few simple two-syllable Infinitives with the change of -овать to -у- and the stress on the endings in the Present tense:

кова́ть — кую́, куёт — ко́ванный   *to forge*
сова́ть — сую́, суёт — (за)со́ванный   *to shove*
жева́ть — жую́, жуёт — жёванный   *to chew*
клева́ть — клюю́, клюёт — (за)клёванный   *to peck*
плева́ть — плюю́, плюёт — (на)плёванный   *to spit*

Also основа́ть — осную́, оснуёт — осно́ванный (pfv.) *to found, base.*

(*d*) Infinitives in -овать/-евать; -изовать; -ировать and -изи-ровать are stressed as follows:

(i) -овать/-евать: Infinitives with the accent on the stem or on -ать are equally common.

Common verbs with accent on the stem (and therefore fixed) include:

бесе́довать	to chat	путеше́ствовать	to travel
ве́ровать	to believe	ра́доваться	to rejoice
де́йствовать	to act	сле́довать	to follow
жа́ловаться	to complain	соверше́нство-	to improve,
же́ртвовать	to sacrifice	вать	perfect
заве́довать	to manage	сове́товать	to advise
зави́довать	to envy	соотве́тство-	to correspond
кома́ндовать	to give orders	вать	to
по́льзоваться	to use	спосо́бствовать	to facilitate
пра́здновать	to celebrate	тре́бовать	to demand
предше́ствовать	to precede	уча́ствовать	to participate
препя́тствовать	to prevent	ца́рствовать	to reign
приве́тствовать	to welcome	чу́вствовать	to feel
про́бовать	to try		

Almost all verbs with suffix **-ствовать** have this stress. Exceptions are **существова́ть** *to exist* and **торжествова́ть** *to celebrate*.

Common verbs with the accent on **-ать** in the Infinitive (and therefore stressed as in §73*b* above) include:

арестова́ть (pfv.)	to arrest	образова́ть*	to form
атакова́ть	to attack	пакова́ть	to pack
балова́ть	to indulge	публикова́ть	to publish
бунтова́ть	to rebel	ревнова́ть	to be jealous
воева́ть	to wage war	рекомендова́ть*	to recommend
волнова́ться	to be agitated	рисова́ть	to sketch
голосова́ть	to vote	существова́ть	to exist
диктова́ть	to dictate	танцева́ть	to dance
интересова́ть	to interest	торгова́ть	to trade
критикова́ть	to criticise	тоскова́ть	to pine
любова́ться	to admire	целова́ть	to kiss
ночева́ть	to spend the night		

Note that the verbs marked * are used both as Imperfectives and Perfectives (but in the Past tense only as Perfectives).

Some verbs of this type are specifically Perfective, and form Imperfectives by adding the suffix **-ывать**, the stress moving back by one syllable on to the **-ов-**, e.g. **арестова́ть — аресто́вывать**; **основа́ть** (§73*c*) — **осно́вывать**. Cf. §70.

Imperfectives are formed in this way also from compounds of verbs of this type, e.g.

завоева́ть (pfv.) *to conquer* — **завоёвывать**

распакова́ть (pfv.) *to unpack* — **распако́вывать**

(ii) **-изовать**: *All* verbs with this suffix have stress on the **-ать** of the Infinitive and change of stress as in §73b above, e.g.

кристаллизова́ть	*to crystallise*	популяризова́ть	*to popularise*
мобилизова́ть	*to mobilise*	реализова́ть	*to realise*
организова́ть	*to organise*	централизова́ть	*to centralise*

The above verbs serve for both aspects.

Note that for some verbs two alternative infinitives exist, one in **-изова́ть**, the other in **-изи́ровать**. They are used indiscriminately. Examples are:

индустриализова́ть or индустриализи́ровать *to industrialise*
стандартизова́ть or стандартизи́ровать *to standardise*

(iii) **-ировать**: A minority of Infinitives with this suffix have the stress on **-ать** (and corresponding stress on **-у-** in the Present tense), e.g.

бомбардирова́ть*	*to bombard*	маршированирова́ть*	*to march*
группирова́ть*	*to group*	меблирова́ть	*to furnish*
командирова́ть	*to send on a mission*	полирова́ть*	*to polish*
лакирова́ть*	*to varnish*	формирова́ть*	*to form*

But most have the accent fixed throughout on the syllable **-ир-**, e.g.

администри́ровать*	*to administer*	реаги́ровать*	*to react*
анализи́ровать	*to analyse*	редакти́ровать*	*to edit*
аплоди́ровать*	*to applaud*	реклами́ровать	*to advertise*
иллюстри́ровать	*to illustrate*	ремонти́ровать	*to repair*
квалифици́ровать	*to qualify*	синтези́ровать	*to synthesise*
констати́ровать	*to state*	телефони́ровать	*to telephone*
констру́ировать*	*to construct*	формули́ровать*	*to formulate*
ликвиди́ровать	*to liquidate*	фотографи́ровать*	*to photograph*
оккупи́ровать	*to occupy*	цити́ровать*	*to quote*
проекти́ровать*	*to design*	эксплуати́ровать	*to exploit*

A few verbs have alternative stress, sometimes differentiating two meanings, e.g. **планирова́ть** *to plan* (*towns*) and **плани́ровать** *to plan work* and also *to glide*.

Of the verbs in the above lists only those marked * are specifically Imperfective; the majority serve for both aspects.

(iv) **-изировать**: All verbs with this suffix have the accent on the syllable **-ир-** throughout all parts, e.g.

гармонизи́ровать	*to harmonise*
драматизи́ровать	*to dramatise*
коллективизи́ровать	*to collectivise*
механизи́ровать	*to mechanise*
специализи́ровать	*to specialise*

These verbs are used for both aspects.

§74. A small number of first conjugation verbs with infinitives in -ать have stress on the endings in the Present tense:

смея́ться — смею́сь, смеётся — (осме́янный)	*to laugh*
соса́ть — сосу́, сосёт — со́санный	*to suck*
дава́ть — даю́, даёт	*to give*
встава́ть — встаю́, встаёт	*to get up*
остава́ться — остаю́сь, остаётся	*to remain*

and other compounds of -става́ть.

Note in this connection compounds of знать forming aspectual pairs in which the Present and Future tenses are differentiated by stress, e.g. узнава́ть/узна́ть *to recognise, find out*, with Present: узнаю́, узнаёт and Future: узна́ю, узна́ет. Similarly признава́ть/призна́ть *to acknowledge, confess*.

§75. Infinitives in -ать of the second conjugation

(*a*) With stem ending in ж, ч, ш and щ:

Most have stress fixed on the endings of the Present tense:

лежа́ть — лежу́, лежи́т — лежа́щий   *to lie*

Similarly:

бежа́ть (бегу́, бежи́т)	*to run*	молча́ть	*to be silent*
дрожа́ть	*to tremble*	мча́ться	*to rush along*
жужжа́ть	*to buzz*	принадлежа́ть	*to belong*
журча́ть	*to murmur, babble*	стуча́ть	*to knock*
		торча́ть	*to protrude*
звуча́ть	*to sound*	треща́ть	*to crackle*
крича́ть	*to shout*	шурша́ть	*to rustle*
лежа́ть	*to lie*		

Only two have mobile stress in the Present tense (on the stem except in the first person singular where it is on the ending), and stress on the stem in the Past participle passive, e.g. держа́ть — держу́, де́ржит — де́ржанный *to hold*, Present participle active — держа́щий. Similarly дыша́ть *to breathe*, with Present part. active дыша́щий.

The Gerund in -a for these verbs is stressed on the ending (except for лёжа *lying*), e.g. стуча́ *knocking*, держа́ *holding* (but see §55).

The verb **слы́шать** *to hear*, having the accent on the stem in the Infinitive, has it fixed there throughout:

слы́шу, слы́шит — слы́шащий — слы́шанный.

(*b*) With stem ending in a vowel: the Present has stress on the endings:

стоя́ть — стою́, стои́т — стой! — стоя́ла	*to stand*
(and its compounds)	
боя́ться — бою́сь, бои́тся — бо́йся! — боя́лась	*to fear*

INFINITIVE IN -еть

§76. Verbs of the **first conjugation** all have stress in the Infinitive on the suffix. There are three different types:

(*a*) Those which retain the stem vowel е in the Present/future tense always have stress on this vowel throughout all forms, e.g.

име́ть — име́ю, име́ет — име́ющий — име́ла — име́я *to have*
Similarly:

греть	*to warm*	**красне́ть**	*to be/turn red*
жале́ть	*to regret*	**уме́ть**	*to know how to*
желте́ть	*to be/turn yellow*	**успе́ть** (pfv.)	*to have time*

Exceptions to this are **ржа́веть** *to rust* and a few uncommon verbs with stress fixed on the stem throughout: **ржа́веет.**

(*b*) **Хоте́ть** *to want* is anomalous, with a change of conjugation and stress in the Present tense:

хоте́ть — хочу́, хо́чет; хоти́м . . . хотя́т — хотя́щий — хоте́ла

(*c*) A few verbs add the first conjugation endings of the Present/future tense directly after the consonant of the stem. One of them has fixed stress:

реве́ть — реву́, ревёт — реве́л, реве́ла   *to roar*

A few others behave like monosyllabic verbs:

тере́ть — тру, трёт — тёр, тёрла — тёрся, тёрлась	*to rub*
умере́ть — умру́, умрёт — у́мер, умерла́, у́мерло,	
у́мерли — у́мерши (pfv.)	*to die*

Other compounds of **-мереть**, e.g. **замере́ть** *to stand still*, '*freeze*' have the same pattern.

Compounds of **пере́ть** (itself used only in colloquial speech in the sense *to go*) fall into two groups: **запере́ть** (pfv.) *to lock* and **отпере́ть** (pfv.) *to unlock* have mobile stress like **умере́ть**, stressing the endings and prefixes in the Past tense and Past participle passive (cf. §§93*b*, 94*b*):

запере́ть — запру́, запрёт — за́пер, заперла́, за́перло,
за́перли — за́пертый/за́перт, заперта́, за́перто (pfv.) *to lock*

Reflexive forms may have stress on the **-ся** and endings of the masculine, neuter and plural in the Past tense (cf. §93*d*):

за́перся or заперся́, заперла́сь, за́перлось or заперло́сь, etc.
Note the participle за́перший(-ся) and gerunds заперев or за́перши, and заперши́сь.

Other compounds of **пере́ть** tend to have the pattern of **тере́ть**, keeping the stress on the stem in most forms, e.g. упере́ть (pfv.) *to rest against, lean*:

Past: упёр, упёрла, упёрло; refl. упёрся, упёрлась, упёрлось
упёртый/упёрт, упёрта, упёрто
упере́в or упёрши; refl. уперши́сь or упёршись.

There is considerable variation in the stress of this and other compounds of **пере́ть**, particularly in colloquial speech.

Оде́ть, наде́ть etc. are dealt with under monosyllabic infinitives below (§95*b*).

§77. Verbs of the second conjugation in -еть follow in general the same patterns as verbs in **-ить**.

(*a*) Only two common verbs of the second conjugation have stress on the stem in the Infinitive, and therefore fixed stress: ви́деть — ви́жу, ви́дит — ви́дящий — ви́дела — ви́денный — ви́дя *to see* and оби́деть (д/ж) (pfv.) *to offend*. Compounds of **ви́деть** like **ненави́деть** *to hate*, have this same pattern.

(*b*) The majority of second conjugation verbs in **-еть** have the stress on the ending in the Infinitive. They fall into two unequal groups:

(i) The majority have stress on all endings in the Present/future tense, e.g. горе́ть — горю́, гори́т — горя́щий — горе́ла — горя́ *to burn*. Similarly:

веле́ть	*to order*	лете́ть(т/ч)	*to fly*
висе́ть(с/ш)	*to hang*	сиде́ть(д/ж)	*to sit*
гляде́ть(д/ж)	*to look*	скрипе́ть(п/пл)	*to squeak, creak*
греме́ть(м/мл)	*to thunder*	храпе́ть(п/пл)	*to snore*
гуде́ть(д/ж)	*to buzz, hoot*	шипе́ть(п/пл)	*to hiss*
звене́ть	*to ring*	шуме́ть(м/мл)	*to make a noise*
кипе́ть(п/пл)	*to boil*		

But note that one compound of **висе́ть** — зави́сеть *to depend* — has stress on the stem throughout.

Two verbs of this type have alternative conjugations: *to shine* блестѣть—блещу́, блести́т or блещу́, бле́щет; and *to whistle* свистѣть—свищу́, свисти́т or свиста́ть—свищу́, сви́щет.

Болѣть in the sense *to be ill* is of first conjugation, болѣю, болѣет but in the sense *to hurt, ache* is second conjugation: боли́т, боля́т.

(ii) Only three have mobile stress in the Present tense and stress on the stem in the Past participle passive: смотрѣть — смотрю́, смо́трит — смотря́щий — смотрѣла — смотря́ *to look*. Similarly вертѣть(т/ч) *to turn* (Past part., e.g. заве́рченный) and терпѣть(п/пл) *to suffer, endure*. The Present participle active of вертѣть is вертя́щий, but of терпѣть — те́рпящий.

INFINITIVE IN -нуть

§78. Stress in these verbs is nearly always fixed, either on the stem or the endings.

§79. Stress is of course always fixed throughout if it falls on the stem in the Infinitive (cf. §60), e.g.

✗ дви́нуть — дви́ну, дви́нет — дви́нул — дви́нутый *to move*. Similarly, e.g.

ки́нуть	to throw	пры́гнуть	to jump
кри́кнуть	to shout	сту́кнуть	to knock
ло́пнуть	to burst	су́нуть	to shove
плю́нуть	to spit	тро́нуть	to touch

All of the above are Perfectives.

All verbs in -нуть having zero ending in the masculine form of the Past tense have stress on the stem throughout:

привы́кнуть — привы́кну, привы́кнет — привы́к, привы́кла, привы́кло, etc. (pfv.) *to become accustomed*.

Similarly, e.g.

вя́знуть	to stick	исче́знуть (pfv.)	to disappear
вя́нуть	to fade, wither	кре́пнуть†	to grow stronger
		мёрзнуть	to freeze
га́снуть	to die out	па́хнуть†	to smell
ги́бнуть†	to perish	прони́кнуть(pfv.)	to penetrate
дости́гнуть ⎫	to achieve,	сты́нуть ⎫	
дости́чь (pfv.) ⎭	reach	сты́ть ⎭	to get cool

Those marked † have in the Past tense masculine either the suffixless form or a form in -л (but in the feminine, neuter and plural only the suffixless form), e.g. пах or па́хнул, па́хла, па́хло, па́хли. Several of the others occur with a masculine Past tense form in -л, but the suffixless form is normal. With prefixes only the suffixless forms occur, e.g. **погиб, окреп**.

§80. Most verbs in **-нуть** even with stress on the ending of the Infinitive have fixed stress on the endings of the Present/future tense, but stress on the stem in the Past participle passive, e.g.

> **вернуть — верну, вернёт — вернул — (за)вёрнутый** (pfv.)
> to return. (This participle means *wrapped up*.)

Similarly, e.g.

вздохнуть	*to sigh*	**отдохнуть**	*to rest*
замкнуть	*to lock*	**подчеркнуть**	*to emphasise*
заснуть	*to fall asleep*	**проснуться**	*to awake*
кивнуть	*to nod*	**улыбнуться**	*to smile*
махнуть	*to wave*	**чихнуть**	*to sneeze*

The only Past participles passive among these examples are **замкнутый** and **подчёркнутый**.

All these verbs are perfectives.

Note the pair of verbs **пахнуть** *to smell* (in group §79 above) and **пахнуть** *to puff* in the present group. ×) also to blow violently

§81. Only five verbs in **-нуть** (and their compounds) have mobile stress in the Present/future tense, and stress on the stem in the Past participle passive. They are:

обмануть (pfv.)	*to deceive*	**тонуть**	*to sink, drown*
помянуть (pfv.)	*to mention*	**тянуть**	*to pull*

тонет

and compounds of **-глянуть**, e.g. **взглянуть** (pfv.) *to glance*, **заглянуть** *to peep, drop in* (although the colloquial verb **глянуть** itself has fixed stress), e.g. **тянуть — тяну, тянет — тянул — тянущий — тянутый**.

INFINITIVE IN **-оть**

§82. In verbs in **-оть** the stress is always on the ending of the Infinitive and the Present tense has mobile stress. The stress varies in the gerund in **-я**.

> **бороться — борюсь, борется — борющийся —**
> **боролся — борясь** to struggle
>
> **колоть — колю, колет — колющий — колол —**
> **коля — колотый** to chop, stab
>
> **молоть — мелю, мелет — молол — мелющий —**
> **молотый** to grind

INFINITIVE IN -ить

§83. The infinitives of verbs in **-ить** mainly have stress on the suffix **-ить,** but some have stress on the stem.

§84. Verbs with the accent not on the ending in the infinitive have stress fixed throughout on the same syllable (cf. §60).

ве́рить — ве́рю, ве́рит — ве́рящий — ве́рила — (у)-ве́ренный
    to believe. (This participle means *convinced.*)

Similarly, dividing according to aspect:

(*a*) Imperfectives, e.g.

беспоко́ить	*to trouble*	по́мнить	*to remember*
ве́рить	*to believe*	по́ртить(т/ч)	*to spoil*
гото́вить(в/вл)	*to prepare*	спо́рить	*to argue*
е́здить(д/ж)	*to travel*	ссо́риться	*to quarrel*
знако́мить(м/мл)	*to acquaint*	ста́вить(в/вл)	*to put*
зна́чить	*to mean*	сто́ить	*to be worth*
кле́ить	*to glue*	стро́ить	*to build*
кра́сить(с/ш)	*to paint*	тра́тить(т/ч)	*to spend*
нра́виться(в/вл)	*to please*	чи́стить(ст/щ)	*to clean*
па́рить	*to steam*		

Note the stress in **сто́ит** *is worth* and **стои́т** *stands* (from **стоя́ть** §75*b*).

(*b*) Perfectives: Note how the stress in these differs from that of the corresponding Imperfectives (given in brackets), e.g.

бро́сить(с/ш)	*to throw*	(броса́ть)
втсре́тить(т/ч)	*to meet*	(встреча́ть)
заста́вить(в/вл)	*to compel*	(заставля́ть)
заме́тить(т/ч)	*to notice*	(замеча́ть)
ко́нчить	*to finish*	(конча́ть)
оста́вить(в/вл)	*to leave*	(оставля́ть)
отве́тить(т/ч)	*to answer*	(отвеча́ть)
отпра́вить(в/вл)	*to send off*	(отправля́ть)
позво́лить	*to permit*	(позволя́ть)
предста́вить(в/вл)	*to present*	(представля́ть)
приба́вить(в/вл)	*to add*	(прибавля́ть)
разру́шить	*to destroy*	(разруша́ть)
уда́рить	*to strike*	(ударя́ть)

In the Imperative these verbs have the reduced ending **-ь** instead of **-и,** unless the stem ends in a group of consonants or a vowel, e.g. **верь, ве́рьте; поста́вь, поста́вьте; брось, бро́сьте; заме́ть, заме́тьте;** but ко́нчи, **ко́нчите; строй, стро́йте.**

This difference in stress between aspects is quite common, but it is not, of course, a standard pattern for all pairs of verbs with Imperfective of first conjugation and Perfective of second conjugation. There are many pairs with stress on the endings in both infinitives, e.g.

повторя́ть/повтори́ть (он повтори́т)
получа́ть/получи́ть (он полу́чит).

§85. Verbs with stress on the suffix -ить in the Infinitive may have fixed stress or mobile stress.

(a) Many verbs in -ить have stress fixed on the endings in the Present/future tense, e.g.

говори́ть — говорю́, говори́т — говоря́щий — говоря́ — говори́ла *to speak.*

The Past Participle passive of such verbs has stress on the suffix -ённый in the long form, moving on to the endings in the feminine, neuter and plural short forms. (The stem consonant is modified as in the first person singular of the Present/future), e.g.

говори́ть — говорённый/говорён, говорена́, говорено́, говорены́
запрети́ть — запрещённый/запрещён, запрещена́, запрещено́, запрещены́.

Similarly, e.g.

благодари́ть	to thank	прости́ть(ст/щ)	to forgive
возврати́ть(т/щ)	to return	(pfv.)	
(pfv.)		реши́ть (pfv.)	to decide
горди́ться(д/ж)	to be proud	роди́ться(д/ж)	to be born
грози́ть(з/ж)	to threaten	сади́ться(д/ж)	to sit down
запрети́ть(т/щ)		случи́ться (pfv.)	to happen
(pfv.)	to forbid	согласи́ться(с/ш)	
звони́ть	to ring	(pfv.)	to agree
ложи́ться	to lie down	сообщи́ть (pfv.)	to announce
обрати́ть(т/щ)(pfv.)	to turn	спеши́ть	to hurry
объясни́ть (pfv.)	to explain	стреми́ться(м/мл)	to aspire
определи́ть (pfv.)	to define	убеди́ть (pfv.)	to convince
освободи́ть(д/ж)		употреби́ть(б/бл)	to use
(pfv.)	to liberate	(pfv.)	
пари́ть	to soar	храни́ть	to keep
повтори́ть (pfv.)	to repeat		

Следи́ть has this pattern, except that the Past participle passive has stress on the stem: (про)-сле́женный.

Note that although **сади́ться** and **ложи́ться** are in this class, the simple verbs (**по-**)**сади́ть**, (**по**)-**ложи́ть** belong to the following class, with mobile stress in the Present/future.

(handwritten in margin: положи́ть)

Роди́ться may have stress on the endings of the Past tense when used as a Perfective: **роди́лся, родила́сь, родило́сь, родили́сь.** The Past participle passive is **рождённый.**

The first person singular of the Future tense of **убеди́ть** is not used. Past participle passive: **убеждённый.**

(*b*) Many other verbs in **-ить** have stress in the Present/future tense moving back on to the stem except in the first personal singular, where it is on the ending. In these verbs the Past participle passive generally has the stress on the stem in all forms, e.g.

> **купи́ть — куплю́, ку́пит — купи́ла — ку́пленный/ку́плен, ку́плена,** etc. *to buy.*

The following list includes most common verbs of this type:

(handwritten in margin: варенный / варёный ?)

буди́ть(д/ж)	to waken	поступи́ть(п/пл)	
вари́ть	to boil	(pfv.)	to act, enter
води́ть(д/ж)	to lead	появи́ться(в/вл)	
вози́ть(з/ж)	to carry	(pfv.)	to appear
дави́ть(в/вл)	to crush	(с-)проси́ть(с/ш)	to ask
дели́ть	to divide	пусти́ть(ст/щ)(pfv.)	to let
жени́ть(-ся)	to marry	руби́ть(б/бл)	to cut, hew
кати́ть(т/ч)	to roll	сади́ть(д/ж)	to set, plant
корми́ть(м/мл)	to feed	свети́ть(т/ч)	to shine
кружи́ть(-ся)	to whirl	серди́ться(д/ж)	to be angry
крути́ть(т/ч)	to turn	служи́ть	to serve
купи́ть(п/пл)(pfv.)	to buy	станови́ться(в/вл)	to become
кури́ть	to smoke	(за)-стрели́ть(pfv.)	to shoot
лечи́ть	to treat, cure	суди́ть(д/ж)	to judge
лови́ть(в/вл)	to catch	(see below)	
люби́ть(б/бл)	to love	тащи́ть	to drag
(из)-мени́ть (pfv.)	to change	торопи́ть(п/пл)	to hasten
(see below)		труди́ться(д/ж)	to toil
моли́ться	to pray	урони́ть (pfv.)	to drop
носи́ть(с/ш)	to carry	учи́ть	to learn, teach
останови́ть(в/вл)	to stop	хвали́ть	to praise
(pfv.)		хвати́ть(т/ч)(pfv.)	to suffice
плати́ть(т/ч)	to pay	ходи́ть (д/ж)	to go
подари́ть (pfv.)	to give, present	цени́ть (see	to value
(по)-ложи́ть (pfv.)	to lay	below)	
получи́ть (pfv.)	to receive	шути́ть(т/ч)	to joke

Положи́ть and сади́ть are of this type, but ложи́ться and сади́ться have stress on the endings throughout the Present tense. Cf. §85a.

Some compounds of води́ть with disyllabic prefixes derived from nouns have fixed stress (although all other compounds of this verb have the mobile stress of the original verb), e.g. перевожу́, перево́дит *translate*, but руковожу́, руководи́т *lead*.

Similarly, some compounds of буди́ть retain the mobile stress, e.g. разбужу́, разбу́дит *to waken* (pfv.), while others have fixed stress on the endings, e.g. возбужу́, возбуди́т *to excite, arouse*; пробужу́, пробуди́т *to awaken, arouse*. The corresponding Past participles passive are разбу́женный, возбуждённый, пробуждённый.

Кружи́ть(-ся) may be stressed like either купи́ть or говори́ть, but the compound окружи́ть *to surround* is always stressed as in §85a, viz. окружи́т — окружённый.

The Imperative plural of these verbs is differentiated from the second person plural of the Present/future by stress, e.g. вы ку́пите — купи́те!; вы но́сите — носи́те!

The Present participle active is usually stressed on the suffix -ящий, even if the third person plural of the Present tense has stress on the stem, e.g. хо́дят — ходя́щий; про́сят — прося́щий. From the verbs in the above list the following are the only participles with stress on the stem: де́лящий, же́нящийся, ле́чащий, лю́бящий, ру́бящий, слу́жащий, та́щащий, це́нящий. Note the difference in stress in у́чащий *teaching* and уча́щийся *a student*.

The Past Participle passive conforms to the rule given at the beginning of this section in the majority of verbs listed, but there are a few exceptions in which the suffix of the participle is stressed and stress is mobile in the short form (cf. §85a). They are суди́ть and its compounds and compounds of дели́ть, свети́ть, -мени́ть and цени́ть; e.g. суждённый/суждён, суждена́, суждено́, etc. Similarly e.g. разделённый *divided*, освещённый *lighted*, изменённый *changed*, and оценённый *estimated, appreciated*.

Compounds of люби́ть with the prefixes воз-, раз-, из-, etc., have stress on the stem in the Past participle passive, e.g. возлю́бленный *beloved*, but the verb влюби́ться (pfv.) *to fall in love* has stress on the suffix of this participle, moving on to the endings in the short forms: влюблённый/влюблён, влюблена́, влюблено́, влюблены́.

The Past participle passive of **заслужи́ть** *to deserve* is normally **заслу́женный**, but as an adjective *honoured* in titles may be **заслужённый**, e.g. **заслу́женный арти́ст** or **заслужённый арти́ст**.

A few other adjectives derived from Past participles passive of the verbs in this group have stress on the suffix, although in the corresponding participles proper, stress is on the stem, e.g. **варёный карто́фель** *boiled potatoes*, **хорошо́ сложённый** *well-built* (*in physique*), **исступлённый** *frenzied*, **учёный** *learned, scholar*; cf. normal participles from these verbs, e.g. **зава́ренный** *scalded*, **сло́женный** *put together*, **обу́ченный** *trained*.

§86. The Present participle passive of all verbs in **-ить** has the same stress as the Infinitive, e.g. **ви́димый, лови́мый, люби́мый.**

The Gerund in **-я/-а** also has this stress, e.g. **говоря́, стро́я, любя́.** The Gerund from **суди́ть** is normally **судя́**, but the form **су́дя** is used in the phrase **су́дя по**, e.g. **су́дя по его́ ви́ду, он бо́лен** *judging by his appearance* ...

§87. Ошиби́ться *to make a mistake* and other compounds of **-шиби́ть** are of first conjugation, with zero ending in the masculine form of the Past tense and stress on the endings of the Present tense, e.g. **ушиби́ть** (pfv.) *to hurt, bruise*: **ушибу́сь, ушибётся — уши́бся, уши́блась — уши́бленный.**

MONOSYLLABIC INFINITIVES (including those in **-ти**)

§88. These verbs, 'irregular' in that they show a great variety of forms, also present most variations of stress, chiefly in the Past tense and Past participle passive.

§89. Monosyllabic verbs fall into two main categories from the point of view both of conjugation and of accentuation: (i) those with the infinitive ending in **-ать, -еть, -ить, -ыть, -уть** and (ii) those with the infinitive ending in **-сть, -зть, -чь, -ти.** These categories are dealt with separately in the section on the Past tense below: §§93-95 and 96-98 respectively.

Present/future tense

§90. All verbs with monosyllabic infinitives except **гнать, мча́ться, спать, дать** and **есть** have first conjugation endings in the Present/future tense and chiefly have these endings stressed throughout this tense as well as in the Imperative, Present participle active and Gerund in **-я** (in the relatively few verbs which have one), e.g.

брать — беру́, берёт — бери́ — беру́щий — беря́   *to take*
жить — живу́, живёт — живи́ — живу́щий — живя́   *to live*
идти́ — иду́, идёт — иди́ — иду́щий — идя́   *to go*

Знать is a regular verb of the first conjugation stressed like чита́ть.

§91. Stress on the stem in the Present/future occurs in the following verbs:

бри́ться (бре́юсь, бре́ется)	*to shave*
быть (бу́ду, бу́дет fut.)	*to be*
дуть (ду́ю, ду́ет)	*to blow*
закры́ть (закро́ю, закро́ет pfv.)	*to close*
(and other compounds of кры́ть)	
лезть (ле́зу, ле́зет)	*to climb*
лечь (ля́гу, ля́жет pfv.)	*to lie down*
мыть (мо́ю, мо́ет)	*to wash*
выть (во́ю, во́ет)	*to howl*
наде́ть (наде́ну, наде́нет pfv.)	*to put on*
(and other compounds of деть)	
сесть (ся́ду, ся́дет pfv.)	*to sit down*
стать (ста́ну, ста́нет pfv.)	*to stand, become, begin*

§92. Mobile stress in the Present/future occurs only in a few verbs with monosyllabic infinitives, viz. some compounds of -ять: приня́ть — приму́, при́мет *to accept*, подня́ть — подниму́, подни́мет *to raise*, снять — сниму́, сни́мет *to take off* (but взять *to take*, заня́ть *to occupy*, and поня́ть *to understand* have stress on the endings, e.g. пойму́, поймёт); and stress is mobile also in стлать — стелю́, сте́лет *to spread*, мочь — могу́, мо́жет *to be able*, and гнать — гоню́, го́нит *to drive, pursue*. Note the stress of the Present participles active: сте́лющий but могу́щий, гоня́щий.

Past tense and Past participle passive of monosyllabic verbs in -ать, -еть, -ить, -уть, -ыть

§93. Monosyllabic infinitives ending in -ать, -еть, -ить, -уть, -ыть.

(*a*) About half of these verbs have fixed stress in the Past tense (and Past participle passive), e.g.

бить — бил, би́ла, би́ло, би́ли   *to beat*

and the other half have the stress on the ending of the feminine form of the Past tense (and Past participle passive) but otherwise on the stem, e.g.

ждать — ждал, ждала́, жда́ло, жда́ли   *to wait*

See the table in §95 for lists.

(*b*) Some monosyllabic verbs in this group when compounded
with prefixes tend to move the accent back on to the prefix in the
masculine, neuter and plural forms of the Past tense, but not in the
feminine, where it remains on the ending, e.g.

жить — жил, жила́, жи́ло, жи́ли } to live
прожи́ть — про́жил, прожила́, про́жило, про́жили }
нача́ть — на́чал, начала́, на́чало, на́чали   to begin

This happens with the prefixes до-, за-, на-, о-, об-, от-, пере-, по-,
под-, при-, про- and у- (but not in the past tense with из-, воз-, and
seldom with раз-, which when stressed becomes роз-) in compounds
of быть (except забы́ть *forget*, with fixed stress), дать, жить, лить,
пить and -ять and in a few other isolated cases, e.g. проби́ть *strike*
(of a clock) (whereas other compounds of бить have fixed stress).
Examples with various prefixes are:

допи́ть — до́пил, допила́, до́пило, до́пили — to drink up
зада́ть — за́дал, задала́, за́дало, за́дали — to set (*a task*)
заня́ть — за́нял, заняла́, за́няло, за́няли — to occupy
наня́ть — на́нял, наняла́, на́няло, на́няли — to hire
ожи́ть — о́жил, ожила́, о́жило, о́жили — to come to life
обня́ть — о́бнял, обняла́, о́бняло, о́бняли — to embrace
отли́ть — о́тлил, отлила́, о́тлило, о́тлили — to pour off, cast
отдать — о́тдал, отдала́, о́тдало, о́тдали — to give up/back
переда́ть — пе́редал, передала́, пе́редало, etc. — to pass, transmit
поня́ть — по́нял, поняла́, по́няло, по́няли — to understand
пода́ть — по́дал, подала́, по́дало, по́дали — to serve, give
подня́ть — по́днял, подняла́, по́дняло, etc. — to raise
приня́ть — при́нял, приняла́, при́няло, etc. — to take, accept
прода́ть — про́дал, продала́, про́дало, etc. — to sell
проли́ть — про́лил, пролила́, про́лило, etc. — to spill
созда́ть — со́здал, создала́, со́здало, etc. — to create
убы́ть — у́был, убыла́, у́было, у́были — to subside

In fact there is a tendency for this pattern to be lost in colloquial
speech, and for many verbs in this category there is a recognised
colloquial variant, with stress on the stem in the masculine, neuter
and plural forms, e.g. пода́л, подала́, пода́ло, пода́ли. (This
applies to most compounds of дать, жить and быть.) Moreover,
for a considerable number of such prefixed verbs there are recognised
'correct' variants, e.g. пе́режил or пережи́л, пережила́, пе́режило
or пережи́ло, пе́режили or пережи́ли. (Most compounds of лить
and пить have these alternatives.)

On the other hand, the basic pattern with stress on the prefixes in masculine, neuter and plural forms is *obligatory* with **нача́ть, поня́ть, приня́ть, заня́ть, наня́ть** and **убы́ть**.

As this basic pattern is hardly ever *wrong*, it can be adhered to for all compounds of these verbs. (Apart from **забы́ть**, verbs in which stress on the stem in these forms has become the norm include: *to tipple* — **подпи́л, подпила́**; *to spill* — **разли́л, разлила́**; *to calm* — **уня́л, уняла́**; and two verbs with prefix **раз-**: *to separate* — **разня́л, разняла́**; and *to drink* (*in a group*) — **распи́л, распила́**, both having colloquial forms with stressed prefix **роз-**, e.g. **ро́знял, разняла́, ро́зняло, ро́зняли**. **Разда́ть** *to distribute* also has this prefix under stress as a regular form: **ро́здал** or **разда́л, раздала́, ро́здало** or **разда́ло**, etc.)

ро́здан [handwritten margin note]

Two senses of **запи́ть** are differentiated by stress in the Past tense: **за́пил, запила́** *to take to drink*, and **запи́л, запила́** *to wash down*.

и́зданный [handwritten margin note]

The prefix **из-** does not take on the accent in any forms of the Past tense, e.g. **изда́ть** — **изда́л, издала́, изда́ло** etc. *to publish*.

Monosyllabic verbs other than **быть, дать, жить, лить, пить** and **-ять** do not as a rule stress prefixes in compounds, but retain the stress pattern of the basic verb, e.g.

собра́ть — собра́л, собрала́, собра́ло, собра́ли	*to collect*
назва́ть — назва́л, назвала́, назва́ло, назва́ли	*to name*
посла́ть — посла́л, посла́ла, посла́ло, посла́ли	*to send*
уби́ть — уби́л, уби́ла, уби́ло, уби́ли	*to kill*
сорва́ть — сорва́л, сорва́ло, сорва́ло, сорва́ли	*to tear off*

The prefix **вы-** of Perfective verbs is of course stressed in all forms, regardless of conjugation, e.g.

вы́мыть — вы́моет — вы́мыл, вы́мыла, etc.	*to wash*
вы́брать — вы́берет — вы́брал, вы́брала, etc.	*to choose*

Prefixes do *not* bear the stress in the Present/future tense (except **вы-**). They retain the stress pattern of the basic verb for this tense, e.g. **прода́м, прода́шь, прода́ст, продади́м**, etc.

(*c*) **Negative particle**: The negative particle **не** takes on the character of a stress-bearing prefix with the masculine, neuter and plural forms of the Past tense of the verbs **быть, жить** and **дать**, e.g.

жил, жила́, жи́ло, жи́ли — не́ жил, не жила́, не́ жило, не́ жили. Similarly **не́ был, не была́; не́ дал, не дала́** (cf. §94*a*). This was formerly much more widespread, e.g. **не́ взял** (archaic).

(*d*) **Reflexive verbs**: All verbs of this group which in the Past tense stress the ending of the feminine form only, when used with the reflexive pronoun stress the endings of the neuter and plural forms also, e.g.

брал, брала́, бра́ло, бра́ли — бра́лся, брала́сь, брало́сь, брали́сь.

Frequently the neuter and plural reflexive forms with stress on the stem are in fact considered permissible alternatives, e.g. **брало́сь** or **бра́лось; рвало́сь** or **рва́лось; звало́сь** or **зва́лось; спало́сь** or **спа́лось; драло́сь** or **дра́лось; гнало́сь** or **гна́лось.** This applies also to compounds of such verbs with prefixes, e.g. **собрало́сь** or **собра́лось; дождало́сь** or **дожда́лось; назвало́сь** or **назва́лось; сорвало́сь** or **сорва́лось.** With other verbs, however, stress on the stem in these forms is considered colloquial, so that e.g. **сбыло́сь, взяло́сь, дало́сь, жило́сь** are standard Russian, while **сбы́лось, взя́лось, да́лось, жи́лось** are colloquial.

In compounds of **дать, жить, лить** and **пить** used as reflexive verbs the prefix loses its stress in the masculine, neuter and plural forms, the stress falling in the masculine form on the stem, in all others on the endings, e.g.

про́дал, продала́, про́дало, про́дали — прода́лся, продала́сь, продало́сь, продали́сь.

Similarly e.g. **передала́сь, передало́сь; раздала́сь, раздало́сь; ужила́сь, ужило́сь** (*to settle down, get on with*)**; отлила́сь, отлило́сь; допила́сь, допило́сь.** Neuter and plural forms of such verbs with stress on the stem are colloquial.

Stress on the endings of the Past tense is *obligatory* in most compounds of **-ять** used as reflexives:

заня́лся, заняла́сь, занялó́сь, заняли́сь

наня́лся, наняла́сь, нанялó́сь, наняли́сь

exception { **обня́лся, обняла́сь, обняло́сь, обняли́сь**
{ **отня́лся, отняла́сь, отняло́сь, отняли́сь**

подня́лся, подняла́сь, подняло́сь, подняли́сь

приня́лся, приняла́сь, приняло́сь, приняли́сь

and also in **уда́ться — уда́лся, удало́сь** *to succeed*, and **нача́ться — начался́, началó́сь** *to begin*. Note the accent on **-ся** in the masculine form of **заня́ться, наня́ться, нача́ться, подня́ться, приня́ться.**

Formerly many other verbs had stress on **-ся** in this form, but it is now considered archaic (e.g. in **дрался́**) except in the above-mentioned verbs. The form for **подня́ться** may be either **подня́лся** or **подня́лся.**

Verbs with fixed stress in the Past tense keep the accent on the stem even when used reflexively, e.g.

оде́ться — оде́лся, оде́лась, оде́лось, оде́лись   *to dress*
умы́ться — умы́лся, умы́лась, умы́лось, умы́лись   *to wash*

§94. (*a*) In the **Past participle passive** the pattern of stress in the short forms is similar to that of the Past tense: verbs with stress on the stem throughout the Past tense have the accent fixed on the stem in the short form, e.g.

бить — бил, би́ла, би́ло, би́ли — би́тый/бит, би́та, би́то, би́ты

while verbs with stress on the ending of the feminine form of the Past tense have the accent on the ending of the feminine short form of the participle, e.g.

звать — звал, звала́, зва́ло, зва́ли — зва́нный/зван, звана́, зва́но, зва́ны

See the table in §95.

Stress moves on to не only with да́нный — не́ дан, не дана́, не́ дано, не́ даны (cf. §93*c*).

(*b*) The tendency to shift the stress on to **prefixes** is here even stronger than in the Past tense, and the long form of the Past participle passive from all verbs with syllabic prefixes stressing the feminine ending in the Past tense, has the stress on the prefix, even if the accent does not fall on the prefix in the Past tense, e.g.

на́чал, начала́, — на́чатый   *begun*
по́днял, подняла́ — по́днятый   *lifted*
про́жил, прожила́ — про́житый   *lived through*
     etc.

with unstressed prefix in the Past tense:

собра́л, собрала́ — со́бранный   *gathered*
назва́л, назвала́ — на́званный   *named*
прогна́л, прогнала́ — про́гнанный   *driven away*
заспа́л, заспала́ — за́спанный   *looking sleepy*

with fixed stress in the Past tense:

согну́л, согну́ла — со́гнутый   *bent*
посла́л, посла́ла — по́сланный   *sent*
узна́л, узна́ла — у́знанный   *recognised*
разостла́л, разостла́ла — разо́стланный   *spread*

This applies even to the prefix из-, which is never stressed in the Past tense, e.g.

избра́л, избрала́ — и́збранный   *selected*
изда́л, издала́ — и́зданный   *published*

Note the position of the accent on пере- in: перебранный *sorted, looked over*; перегнанный *driven somewhere else, distilled*; пересланный *sent*, etc. Exceptions are переданный *passed, transferred* and перенятый *adopted, imitated*.

Note the difference in stress between the participle приданный *added*, and the noun приданое *dowry*.

Compounds of быть, дать, -ять, жить, лить and пить which stress the prefix in the masculine, neuter and plural forms of the Past tense may have stress on the prefix in the long form of this participle, e.g. in переданный, поднятый and other compounds of дать and -ять; or have the choice of stress either on the prefix or on the stem, e.g. пережитый or пережитый; налитый or налитый; допитый or допитый; добытый or добытый; and in most other compounds of жить, лить and пить. In some compounds of these verbs the form with stress on the stem has in fact become the norm, e.g. разлитый, запитый. Раздать *distribute* has the forms розданный/роздан, раздана, роздано, розданы (cf. Past tense §93*b*).

(*c*) In the **predicative form**, participles with stressed prefixes follow two patterns: either they retain the accent on the prefix in all the short forms (even if in the Past tense the feminine ending is stressed), e.g.

собранный/собран, собрана, собрано, собраны	*gathered*
названный/назван, названа, названо, названы	*named*
посланный/послан, послана, послано, посланы	*sent*

or they stress the prefix in the masculine, neuter and plural forms, but the ending in the feminine form, e.g.

начатый/начат, начата, начато, начаты	*begun*
занятый/занят, занята, занято, заняты	*occupied*

Stress either on the prefix or the stem is permissible in the feminine form *sold*: продана or продана; and in many compounds of жить, лить and пить having this alternative in the long form, the same alternatives exist for the short form, e.g. отлит or отлит, отлита, отлито or отлито, etc.

Note the Past participle passive of развить — развит, развита, развито, развиты, with the two long forms развитый or развитой in the general sense *developed*, but only развитой in the sense *well-developed* (of a child, industry, etc.). Similarly, in addition to the participle занятый *occupied*, there is the adjective занятой *busy* which has no short forms.

(d) Verbs in which the prefix is not stressed in the Past participle passive include all those in table §95a and b marked fixed. They have the stress pattern of the basic participle without a prefix. Examples are:

нажа́тый/нажа́т, нажа́та, etc.	*pressed; reaped*
измя́тый/измя́т, измя́та, etc.	*crumpled*
уби́тый/уби́т, уби́та, etc.	*killed*
закры́тый/закры́т, закры́та, etc.	*closed*
умы́тый/умы́т, умы́та, etc.	*washed*
забы́тый/забы́т, забы́та, etc.	*forgotten*
оде́тый/оде́т, оде́та, etc.	*clothed*
наду́тый/наду́т, наду́та, etc.	*inflated*

§95. Table of verbs with monosyllabic infinitives in -ать, -еть, -ить, -уть, -ыть.

Abbreviations used:

Present/future tense

Stem of Present/future is given only if it differs from that of the Infinitive.

ёт means that the endings are of the first conjugation, stressed, e.g. зову́, зовёт.

mobile means that stress is on ending in first person singular, but on stem in other parts.

ит means endings are of second conjugation.

stem means the stress throughout the tense is on the stem.

Past tense and Past participle passive

á means that stress is on the stem in masc., neuter and plural forms, on ending in fem. form (and that with the reflexive pronoun all endings in the Past tense *may* be stressed, cf. §93d).

fixed means that stress is on stem in all forms (even with prefixes).

† marks verbs which may move stress on to prefixes in Past tense (cf. §93b).

* marks participles which are formed only with prefixes: stress on prefix unless otherwise indicated (cf. §94b).

— means the participle does not exist.

т- means participle has suffix -тый not -нный, e.g. закры́тый *closed*.

(a) Past tense with stress on feminine ending

		Present	Past	Past part. pass.	
1.	врать	ёт	á	*	*to tell lies*
2.	ждать	ёт	á	*	*to wait*
3.	лгать (лгу, лжёт)	ёт	á	*	*to tell lies*
4.	рвать	ёт	á	*	*to tear*
5.	ткать (тку, ткёт)	ёт	á or fixed	*	*to weave*
6.	брать бер-	ёт	á	*	*to take*

брать X врать

			Present	Past	Past part. pass.	
7.	драть	дер-	ёт	á	*	to tear
8.	звать	зов-	ёт	á	á	to call
9.	гнить	гни-	ёт	á	—	to rot
10.	вить	вь-	ёт	á	т-á	to twist
11.	лить	ль-	ёт	á†	т-á*	to pour
12.	пить	пь-	ёт	á†	т-á*	to drink
13.	жить	жив-	ёт	á†	*	to live
14.	плыть	плыв-	ёт	á	—	to swim
15.	слыть	слыв-	ёт	á	—	to have a name as/for
16.	взять	возьм- (pfv.)	ёт	á	т-á	to take
17.	снять	сним- (pfv.)	mobile	á	т-á	to take off
18.	спать	(п/пл)	ит	á	*	to sleep
19.	гнать	гон-	mobile -ит	á	*	to drive
20.	быть	буд-	stem	á†	*	to be
21.	дать (pfv.)		irreg.	á†	á	to give

(b) Past tense with stress fixed on stem

			Present	Past	Past part. pass.	
1.	гнуть		ёт	fixed	т-*	to bend
2.	льнуть		ёт	fixed	—	to adhere
3.	слать	шл-	ёт	fixed	*	to send
4.	жать	жм-	ёт	fixed	т-fixed*	to press
5.	жать	жн-	ёт	fixed	т-fixed*	to reap
6.	мять	мн-	ёт	fixed	т-fixed*	to crush
7.	бить	бь-	ёт	fixed	т-fixed*	to beat
8.	петь	по-	ёт	fixed	т-fixed*	to sing
9.	шить	шь-	ёт	fixed	т-fixed*	to sew
10.	дуть	дý-	stem	fixed	т-fixed*	to blow
11.	брить	брé-	stem	fixed	т-fixed*	to shave
12.	выть	вó-	stem	fixed	—	to howl
13.	крыть	крó-	stem	fixed	т-fixed*	to cover
14.	мыть	мó-	stem	fixed	т-fixed*	to wash
15.	рыть	рó-	stem	fixed	т-fixed*	to dig
16.	забы́ть	-бýд-(pfv.)	stem	fixed	т-fixed	to forget
17.	деть	дéн-	stem	fixed	т-fixed*	to put
18.	стать	стáн-	stem	fixed	—	to become
19.	знать	знá-	stem	fixed	*	to know
20.	стлать	стел-	mobile	fixed	*	to spread
21.	мчáться		ит	fixed	—	to rush along

(c) **With prefixes** (cf. §§93*b*, 94*b*)

prefix means that in the form concerned stress is on prefix throughout.
prefix -á means stress is on prefix in long form, masc., neut., and plural
short forms but on ending in fem. short form.

1. (со)врать	ёт	á	*prefix*	*to lie*
2. (про)ждать	ёт	á	*prefix*	*to wait*
3. (со)рвать	ёт	á	*prefix*	*to tear*
4. (со)ткать	ёт	á	*prefix*	*to weave*
5. (со)брать	ёт	á	*prefix*	*to gather*
6. (со)драть	ёт	á	*prefix*	*to tear*
7. (на)звать	ёт	á	*prefix*	*to name*
8. (про)спать	ит	á	*prefix*	*to sleep*
9. (у)гнать	*mobile*-ит	á	*prefix*	*to drive away*
10. (со)гнуть	ёт	*fixed*	*prefix*	*to bend*
11. (по)слать	ёт	*fixed*	*prefix*	*to send*
12. (у)знать	*stem*	*fixed*	*prefix*	*to know*
13. (разо)стлать	*mobile*	*fixed*	*prefix*	*to spread out*
14. (про)лить	ёт	*(prefix)*-á	*(prefix)*-á	*to spill*
15. (до)пить	ёт	*(prefix)*-á	*(prefix)*-á	*to drink up*
16. (про)жить	ёт	*(prefix)*-á	*(prefix)*-á	*to live*
17. поня́ть пойм-	ёт	*prefix*-á	*prefix*-á	*to understand*
18. заня́ть займ-	ёт	*prefix*-á	*prefix*-á	*to occupy*
19. (про)дать	*irregular*	*prefix*-á	*prefix*-á	*to sell*
20. нача́ть начн-	ёт	*prefix*-á	*prefix*-á	*to begin*
21. подня́ть -ним-	*mobile*	*prefix*-á	*prefix*-á	*to lift*
22. приня́ть прим-	*mobile*	*prefix*-á	*prefix*-á	*to accept*
23. прибы́ть	*stem*	*prefix*-á	—	*to arrive*
24. забы́ть	*stem*	*fixed*	*fixed*	*to forget*

Past tense and past participle passive of verbs in -ти, -сть, -зть, -чь

§96. *(a)* The Past tense of most of these verbs has stress on the stem
in the masculine form and on the endings in the feminine, neuter and
plural forms, whether reflexive or not, e.g.

нести́ — нёс, несла́, несло́, несли́   *to carry*
приобрести́—приобрёл, приобрела́, приобрело́, etc. *to obtain*

Some verbs have stress fixed on the stem in the Past tense, e.g.

класть — клал, кла́ла, кла́ло, кла́ли   *to lay*
упа́сть — упа́л, упа́ла, упа́ло, упа́ли   *to fall*

See the table in §98 for lists.

Note the two meanings of **сечь** differentiated in the Past tense by
stress: сек, секла́, секло́, секли́ *to cut*, but сек, се́кла, се́кло,
се́кли *to flog*. **Сечь, есть, лезть** and **сесть** are unusual in this
group in having the vowel **e** unmodified in the masculine form of the

Past tense, whereas most of the others modify **e** to **ё** under stress in this form.

(*b*) **Stress does not move on to prefixes** in compounds of these verbs, e.g.

перевести́—перевёл, перевела́, перевело́, etc. (pfv.) *to translate*
проче́сть—прочёл, прочла́, прочло́, прочли́ (pfv.) *to read*

The only exception is прокля́сть (pfv.) *to curse*, with Past tense про́клял, прокляла́, про́кляло, про́кляли.

§97.

The Past participle passive of verbs in **-ти,-сть**, **-зть**, and **-чь** ends in **-енный**. In verbs with stress on the endings in the Past tense (the majority) the stress falls on this suffix, the **e** being modified to **ё**, and in the short form the accent moves on to the endings in the feminine, neuter and plural forms (cf. some verbs in **-ить** §85*a*), e.g.

нести́—несё́нный/несё́н, несена́, несено́, несены́   *carried*
проче́сть—прочтё́нный/прочтё́н, прочтена́, прочтено́,
прочтены́ (pfv.)   *read*

In verbs with stress on the stem in the Past tense the accent remains on the stem in all forms of the Past participle passive, e.g.

укра́сть—укра́денный/укра́ден, укра́дена,
укра́дено, etc.   *stolen*
съесть—съе́денный/съе́ден, съе́дена, съе́дено, etc.   *eaten*

The accent does not move on to the prefix in the Past participle passive of verbs in this group, with the exception of прокля́сть *to curse* (cf. §96*b* above) with про́клятый/про́клят, проклята́, про́клято, про́кляты (cf. the adjective *damned* про́клятый).

Compounds of идти́ show two patterns:

на́йденный/на́йден, на́йдена, на́йдено, на́йдены   *found*
про́йденный/про́йден, про́йдена, про́йдено, про́йдены *passed*

but

перейдё́нный/перейдё́н, перейдена́, перейдено́, etc.   *crossed*
обойдё́нный/обойдё́н, обойдена́, обойдено́, etc.   *gone round,
avoided*

§98. Table of verbs with Infinitive in -ти, -сть, -зть, -чь

First person sing. of Present/future is given only where stem of 1st sing. and 3rd pl. differs from that of 3rd sing. and remainder of tense, e.g. течь — теку́, течёшь, течёт . . . теку́т

Stem of Past part. pass. is the same as that of 3rd sing. of Present.

ён means that the participle has the suffix **-ённый** and that the stress moves on to the endings in the fem., neut. and plur. short forms, e.g. спасён, спасена́, спасено́, спасены́.

* means that the participle is formed only with prefixes.
— means that the participle does not exist.

(a) Past tense and Past participle passive with stress on all endings

	Present	Past	Past part. pass.	
везти́	везёт	вёз,везла́,о́,и́	-ён*	to carry, take
нести́	несёт	нёс,несла́,о́,и́	-ён*	to carry, take
пасти́	пасёт	пас,пасла́,о́,и́	-ён	to pasture, tend
спасти́ (pfv.)	спасёт	спас,спасла́,о́,и́	-ён	to save
ползти́	ползёт	полз/ла́,о́,и́	—	to crawl
трясти́	трясёт	тряс/ла́,о́,и́	-ён*	to shake
расти́	растёт	рос/ла́,о́,и́	—	to grow
наблюсти́(pfv.)	-блюдёт	-блю́л/а́,о́,и́	-ён*	to observe
вести́	ведёт	вёл,вела́,о́,и́	-ён*	to lead
мести́	метёт	мёл,мела́,о́,и́	-ён	to sweep
плести́	плетёт	плёл/а́,о́,и́	-ён*	to plait
приобрести́ (pfv.)	-бретёт	-брёл/а́,о́,и́	-ён*	to obtain
цвести́	цветёт	цвёл/а́,о́,и́	—	to flower
грести́	гребёт	грёб/ла́,о́,и́	—	to row
клясть	клянёт	клял/а́,о́,и́	§97*	to curse
прочесть(pfv.)	-чтёт	-чёл,-чла́,о́,и́	-ён*	to read
привле́чь (pfv.)	-влеку́, -влечёт	-влёк/ла́,о́,и́	-ён*	to attract
отре́чься (pfv.)	-реку́сь, -речётся	-рёк/ла́,о́,и́	-ён*	to renounce
печь	пеку́,печёт	пёк/ла́,о́,и́	-ён	to bake
сечь	секу́,сечёт	сек/ла́,о́,и́	-ён*	to cut
течь	теку́,течёт	тёк/ла́,о́,и́	—	to flow
бере́чь	берегу́, бережёт	берёг/ла́,о́,и́	-ён*	to preserve
пренебре́чь (pfv.)	-брегу́, -брежёт	-брёг/ла́,о́,и́	-ён*	to neglect
запря́чь (pfv.)	запрягу́, запряжёт	-пря́г/ла́,о́,и́	-ён*	to harness
стере́чь	стерегу́, стережёт	стерёг/ла́,о́,и́	-ён*	to guard
жечь	жгу,жжёт	жёг, жгла,о,и	-ён*	to burn
идти́	идёт	шёл,шла,о,и	§97*	to go
лечь (pfv.)	ля́гу, ля́жет	лёг/ла́,о́,и́	—	to lie down
мочь	могу́, мо́жет	мог/ла́,о́,и́	—	to be able

(b) Past tense with stress fixed on stem

грызть	грызёт	грыз, гры́зла	stem*	to gnaw
класть	кладёт	клал, кла́ла	stem*	to lay
красть	крадёт	крал, кра́ла	stem*	to steal
упа́сть (pfv.)	упадёт	упа́л, упа́ла	—	to fall
прясть	прядёт	прял/пря́ла	stem	to spin
сечь	секу́,сечёт	сек, се́кла	stem	to flog
стричь	стригу́, стрижёт	стриг, стри́гла	stem*	to clip, shear
се́сть (pfv.)	ся́дет	сел, се́ла	—	to sit down
лезть	ле́зет	лез, ле́зла	—	to climb
есть	irregular	ел, е́ла	(-е́денный)	to eat
надое́сть (pfv.)	надое́м, etc.	надое́л/а	—	to bore

(handwritten in right margin: книга упа́ла на по...)

Past participle active

§99. With monosyllabic verbs in **-ать, -еть, -ить, -уть, -ыть,** this is derived from the infinitive and has the stress of the infinitive, e.g.

ждать — жда́вший	*waiting*
прожи́ть — прожи́вший	*having lived*
собра́ть — собра́вший	*having collected*
вы́брать — вы́бравший	*having chosen*

With verbs in **-сть, -зть, -чь, -ти** the stem of this participle is in most cases that of the Present tense. It is without the **-в** characteristic of this form in other verbs, and stress is on the stem (an **e**, as in the Past tense, usually becoming **ё** under the stress), e.g.

нести́ — несёт — нёсший	*carrying*

But four such verbs and their compounds have **ё** in the Past tense, but **e** in this participle:

вести́ — ведёт — ве́дший	*leading*
приобрести́ — приобретёт — приобре́тший	*having obtained*

and similarly **расцве́тший, пренебре́гший.**

The following verbs have the stem of the Past tense in this participle:

расти́ — рос — ро́сший	*growing*
жечь — жёг — жёгший	*burning*
идти́ — шёл — ше́дший	*going*
есть — ел — е́вший	*eating*
класть — клал — кла́вший	*laying*
клясть — клял — кля́вший	*cursing*
сесть — сел — се́вший	*having sat down*

Gerunds

§100. The Gerund in **-я** for both types of monosyllabic verb (insofar as it is used at all) has stress on the ending, e.g.

зовя́	*calling*	плывя́	*swimming*	пройдя́	*having passed*
неся́	*carrying*	кладя́	*laying*		

The Gerund in **-в**, **-вши** from infinitives in **-ать**, **-еть**, **-ить**, **-уть** and **-ыть**, and from such verbs in **-сть** as possess it, has the stress of the infinitive, e.g. **ждав** *waiting*, **нача́в** *having begun*, **вы́пив** *having drunk*, **се́вши** *having sat down*.

The Gerund in **-ши** from infinitives in **-ти**, **-сть**, **-зть**, **-чь** (where it exists) has stress on the stem, e.g. **привлёкши** *having attracted*, **испёкши** *having baked*.

CHAPTER 8

STRESS IN CONNECTED SPEECH

§101. Although any monosyllable in isolation is stressed, and any word of two or more syllables in isolation has one stressed syllable and one or more relatively unstressed, within a sentence there is a whole range of stress, from very strongly emphasised words to those which are scarcely heard at all. In such a sentence as **Она́ се́ла за стол и ста́ла говори́ть с на́ми** for instance, an accent is printed over the stressed syllable of every word of two or more syllables. In the case of **она** and **нами**, however, these whole words are relatively unstressed within the whole pattern of the sentence, their stressed syllables being given much less emphasis than the stressed syllables of **села** or **говорить**. This sentence can be broken up into separate units, each like an isolated word having its pattern of one strongly stressed syllable and other more or less unstressed syllables:

Она‿се́ла / за‿стол / и ста́ла / говори́ть с‿нами.

Within each of these phrases something similar to the general laws of stress and pronunciation of individual words applies. For instance the first phrase is pronounced as a whole, like a word with an initial unstressed **o** and an unstressed **a** in the syllable immediately preceding the stress: [anaˈsɛlə] (cf. §1*b*). The second phrase is similar: [zaˈstɔl], but if **за** were followed by a longer word with the accent falling one or more syllables later, it would then be pronounced with the neutral vowel [ə], e.g. **за прила́вок** *behind the counter* [zəpr̩ɪˈlavək]. In the last phrase however, with stress on **говори́ть**, **с нами** would not rhyme with, e.g. **ни́тками** *threads* (instr.), since its vowel **a** is not reduced to [ə], i.e. [ˈn̩itkəmɪ] but [gəvaˈr̩it̩ snamɪ]. **С нами** has in fact a kind of secondary stress. If the subject of the sentence were masculine: **он сел**, the first phrase, although pronounced as a single unit from the point of view of stress, would not resemble phonetically e.g. the word **отде́л** *department* [adˈdɛl], because the unstressed **o** of **он** is never 'reduced' to [a], but always pronounced [ɔ]: [ɔnˈsɛl]. This is true even when **он** is in a very 'unstressed' position, e.g. at the end of a sentence: **Я приду́ за́втра, – сказа́л он** [skaˈzalɔn].

Thus pronouns, however relatively unstressed in the sentence, do not modify their vowels entirely in accordance with the general rules for unstressed vowels.

Some other words, however, are purely proclitic or enclitic (i.e. attached before or after an independent word and pronounced as if

forming an integral part of it). Such words include most conjunctions, particles and prepositions.

§102. Conjunctions. и, а, но, да, и́ли, ни, что, что́бы are unstressed
and usually pronounced as one phonetic unit with the word preceding
or following, e.g.

Ири́на и я́   [ɪˈɽinəiˈja]
Он не инжене́р, а врач   [aˈvratʃ] or [əˈvratʃ]
Зна́ю, да не скажу́   [dəɳɪskaˈʒu]
С лимо́ном или с молоко́м?   [ɪl̡ɪsməlaˈkɔm]
Я не зна́ю ни его́ ни её   [ɳɪjɪˈvɔɳɪjɪˈjɔ]

In most phrases in which ни is used along with pronouns (кто, что,
ско́лько, како́й, etc.) and adverbs (как, где, куда́, когда́, etc.)
in the sense *whoever, whatever, whenever*, etc., it is unstressed, e.g.

Кто́ ни придёт	*Whoever comes*
Кто́ бы ни пришёл	*Whoever may come*
Куда́ он ни пойдёт	*Wherever he goes*
Куда́ бы он ни пошёл	*Wherever he may go*

But in fixed phrases with то and the past tense of быть, ни is stressed,
e.g.

Кто́ бы то ни́ был	*Whoever it may be*
Что́ бы то ни́ было	*Whatever it may be*
Где́ бы то ни́ было	*Wherever it may be*

But note the phrase **Во что́ бы то ни ста́ло** *at any price*.

It is only in their function as conjunctions that что and что́бы
are unstressed, e.g.

Он сказа́л, что придёт   [ɔnskaˈzal ʃtəpɽɪˈdɔt]
Я хочу́, чтобы он пришёл   [jaxaˈtʃu ʃtəbɪɔnpɽɪˈʃɔl]

As a pronoun, however, что is stressed, e.g.

Я зна́ю, что́ он ска́жет   [jaˈznaju ˌʃtɔɔnˈskaʒət]
Дам тебе всё, что́ бы ты ни проси́л   [ˈfʂɔ ˌʃtɔbitiɳɪpraˈʂil]

In fact even the unstressed conjunction что is sometimes pronounced
[ʃtɔ].

Но is unstressed, but usually pronounced [nɔ], e.g.

Ста́рый, но краси́вый дом   [nɔkraˈʂivəjˈdɔm]

It may be 'reduced' to [nə], but never to [na].

As a conjunction, **то** is always pronounced [tɔ] and may have
secondary stress, e.g.

(unstressed) **Если не хоти́те, то мне всё равно́** [tɔˈmɳɛfʂɔravˈnɔ]
(with secondary stress) **Шёл то дождь, то снег** [tɔˈdɔʃtʃ tɔˈsɳɛk]

As a pronoun **то** is relatively stressed and pronounced with [ɔ], e.g.

Скажу́ то́, что зна́ю [ˌtɔʃtəˈznaju]; **то́ есть** [ˈtɔjɪʂt]. [что то-есть)

Conjunctions with two or more syllables have secondary stress, e.g.

Éсли зна́ешь, скажи́	*If you know tell me.*
Говоря́т, бу̀дто он уже́ здесь	*He's said (supposed) to be here already.*
Скажи́те мне, когда̀ он придёт	*Tell me when he comes.*
Пойду́, потому̀ что обеща́л	*I'll come because I promised.*

§103. The following **particles** are always unstressed:

же	**Он же сказа́л, что придёт**	[ɔnʒəskaˈzal]
		But he said he would *come.*
бы	**Éсли бы я знал, я пришёл бы**	[ˌjesʲlʲɪbʲɪjaˈznal japrʲɪˈʃɔlbʲ]
		If I had known I should have come.

Both **бы** and **же** are habitually so completely unstressed that they are often pronounced and sometimes written as **б** and **ж** respectively after vowels. They then become 'final consonants' and are therefore pronounced unvoiced as **п** and **ш**, e.g. **Éсли б я знал** [ˈjesʲlʲɪp]; **Он пошёл, чтоб узна́ть** [ʃtəpuˈznaṭ]; **Где́ ж он?** [ˈgdɛʃɔn]; **Ну, так что ж?** [ˈʃtɔʃ].

уж	**Кто кто, а о́н уж до́лжен знать**	[aˈɔnuʃ ˈdɔlʒən ˈznaṭ]
		Whoever else may, he should know
ли	**Вы зна́ете, до́ма ли он?**	[ˈdɔməlʲɪon]
		Do you know whether he is at home?
ведь	**Ведь это не пе́рвый раз**	[yɪtʲˈɛtənɪˈpɛrvəjras]
		This isn't the first *time*
-то	see §48.	
-таки	**Всё-таки мне ка́жется...**	[ˈfʂɔtəkʲɪmnʲeˈkaʒətsə]
		Still it seems to me...
-ка	**Погляди́-ка** [pəglʲɪˈdʲikə]	*Have a look.*

§104. While **не** is usually unstressed, it does bear the accent in some indefinite and negative pronouns and adverbs (see §47) and in conjunction with the past tense (and past participle passive) of a few verbs (see §§93c and 94a).

§105. Most **prepositions** are entirely proclitic, fusing completely with the following word and being pronounced as its first letter or syllable, e.g. **к отцу́** [kaˈttsu]; **на столе́** [nəstaˈlʲɛ]; **по у́лице** [paˈulʲɪtsi]; **во всех** [vaˈfʂɛx]; **под столо́м** [pətstaˈlɔm]; **обо мне** [abaˈmnʲɛ]; **из-за стола́** [ɪzzəstaˈla].

The disyllabic prepositions **пе́ред** *before*, **че́рез** *across*, and **ме́жду** *between*, may be unstressed or relatively stressed, e.g. **перед до́мом** [pɪɾɪdˈdɔməm] or [ˌpɛɾɪdˈdɔməm].

But some, mainly disyllabic, prepositions preserve their identity as individual words and retain their independent phonetic form, even though they are relatively unstressed, e.g. **после войны́** [poṣḷɪvajˈnɨ] *after the war*; **вдоль у́лицы** [vdoḷˈuḷɪtsɨ] *along the street*; **кроме того́** [krɔmɪtaˈvɔ] *moreover*. Similarly **сквозь** *through*; **ми́мо** *past*; **о́коло** *about, near*; **вокру́г** *around*; **напро́тив** *opposite* (and other prepositions which are basically adverbs, like **вме́сто** *instead*, **накану́не** *on the eve of*).

§106. Although normally most prepositions are entirely unstressed, in a certain number of phrases consisting of preposition plus noun or preposition plus numeral, the accent has moved completely off the noun or numeral on to the preposition, e.g. **за́ город** *out of town*, **на́ ночь** *for a night*. This takes place only with monosyllables and forms of the noun or numeral having the accent on the first syllable.

The prepositions which act in this way are **на, за, под, об, по, из, от, до** and less frequently **без, у, со**. They combine in this way with:

(*a*) Some common masculine nouns of one syllable or having the accent on the first syllable, a few neuter nouns with stress on the first syllable, and some numerals. The most common combinations are given below.

(i) With **на** in the accusative.

Ле́том мы е́здили на́ море [ˈnaməɾə] *In summer we went to the seaside.*

Доста́вка на́ дом [ˈnadəm] *Delivery to the house.*

Он положи́л ковёр на́ пол [ˈnapəl] *He put the carpet on the floor.*

Он на́ год ста́рше меня́ [ˈnagət] *He's a year older than I am.* Similarly **на́ берег, на́ вечер, на́ волос, на́ день, на́ мост, на́ нос, на́ угол, на́ смех, на́ поле, на́ ухо.**

Also with numerals of one syllable and some of two syllables with stress on the first syllable, especially in multiplication and division and comparison, e.g. **раздели́ть на́ восемь** *divide by eight*, **на́ сорок** *by forty* (but not when units are expressed: **на со́рок пять** *by forty-five*). So with **два/две, три, пять** to **де́сять, со́рок, сто** (but *not* **два́дцать, три́дцать, се́мьдесят, во́семьдесят, две́сти, три́ста** and **ты́сяча**).

Она́ на́ два го́да ста́рше *She is two years older* (comparison), but **Он опозда́л на три́ мину́ты** *He was three minutes late.*

(ii) With **за** in the accusative.

Дёргать кого-либо за́ волосы	*To pull someone's hair.*
Зу́б за́ зуб	*A tooth for a tooth.*

Similarly за́ год, за́ день, за́ нос.

And with the same numerals as in (i) above, e.g. Ему́ за́ сорок *He's over forty*, За́ три го́да до войны́ *Three years before the war.*

(iii) With **за** in the accusative or instrumental.

Они́ живу́т за́ городом.	*They live out of town.*
В воскресе́нье мы е́здили за́ город.	*On Sunday we went into the country.*

Similarly за́ угол, за́ углом, за́ море, за́ морем, за́ поле, за́ полем.

(iv) With **под** in the accusative or instrumental.

Ему́ по́д сорок.	*He's close on forty.*
По́д вечер.	*Towards evening.*

Similarly по́д носом, по́д полом.

(v) With **об** in the accusative.

Стака́н разби́лся о́б пол.	*The glass smashed on the floor.*

(vi) With **по** in the dative.

Мы шли по́ лесу.	*We walked through the wood.*

Similarly по́ лугу, по́ мосту, по́ носу, по́ полу; по́ морю, по́ полю, по́ уху, по́ уши.

Also in the accusative with some numerals:

Фе́рмер дал ма́льчикам по́ три я́блока.	*The farmer gave the boys three apples each.*

So по́ два, по́ три, по́ сто 2/3/100 *each* (but по одному́ *one each*, по четы́ре *four each*, по пя́ть or по пяти́ (dat.) etc. *five each*, etc.).

(vii) With **из, от, до, без** in the genitive case. Here many masculine nouns have the archaic genitive ending **-у**.

Он вы́шел и́з дому.	*He left the house.*
Час о́т часу не ле́гче.	*Things don't get any better.*
Покати́ться со́ смеху.	*To rock with laughter.*
бе́з году неде́ля	*for a short time* (ironically)

Similarly и́з виду, и́з году, и́з лесу, и́з носу; о́т году, о́т роду; до́ дому, до́ полу, до́ ста; со́ ста.

(b) Some feminine nouns ending in -ь act in this way, e.g.

Мы останови́лись на́ ночь в лесу́.	*We stopped for the night in the wood.*
Он лежа́л при́ смерти.	*He lay on the point of death.*
Пропа́сть бе́з вести.	*To be missing (without tidings).*
Бе́з четверти ше́сть.	*A quarter to six.*

Similarly за́ ночь, на́смерть (*to death*), до́ ночи, до́ смерти.

(c) Some common feminine nouns with stress on the first syllable in the accusative singular (and nominative plural) combine:

(i) With на and за in the accusative.

гора́ — го́ру — на́ гору	*up the hill (we went)* (cf. (*we sat*) *on the hill*: на горе́)
Он схвати́л её за́ руку.	*He seized her by the hand.*

Similarly with вода́—во́ду, нога́—но́гу, спина́—спи́ну, зима́—зи́му, душа́—ду́шу, стена́—сте́ну, голова́—го́лову. And with на only: сторона́—сто́рону, доска́—до́ску. Also in the plural, e.g. на́ руки, за́ руки, за́ спины.

(ii) With под and об (*against*) in the accusative.

Мы шли по́д гору.	*We walked downhill.*
Он разби́л ча́шку об стену.	*He broke the cup against the wall.*

Similarly под ногу, под ноги, под руку, под руки, под голову, рука́ об руку.

§107. In fact these usages are not always essential in modern Russian, and there is a tendency to use instead the 'normal' forms of the noun in such phrases, e.g. на бе́рег, на до́м, на по́ле, на де́сять, на со́рок, на мо́ст, за мо́рем, за по́лем, за со́рок, под ве́чер, по ле́су, из го́да, из до́ма, из ле́са, от го́да, до до́ма, под го́лову, об спи́ну, etc.

There is sometimes a difference in meaning between the two variants, e.g.

Он вы́шел и́з дому	*He left home (his own house).*
Рабо́тник вы́шел из до́ма	*The workman came out of the house (not his house).*
Он живёт за́ городом	*He lives in the country.*
За го́родом лес	*Beyond the town there is a forest (on the far side of the town).*

The form with stress on the preposition is less literal, and since it forms a more closely fused phrase, it is almost adverbial in meaning (cf. §57), while the individuality of meaning of the preposition and noun is clearer in the 'normal' form. Therefore stress on the preposition is normal in such definitely adverbial phrases as **под гору** *downhill*, **рука́ о́б руку** *hand in hand*, **на́ ночь** *for the night*, (**шепта́ть**) **на́ ухо** (*to whisper*) *in someone's ear*, **на́смерть** *to death*, and **во́время** *in time* (cf. **во вре́мя войны́** *during the war*). Some fixed phrases also retain stress on the preposition, e.g. **зуб за́ зуб** *a tooth for a tooth*; **час о́т часу не ле́гче** *things don't get any better*; **я о́т- роду не вида́л ничего́ подо́бного** *I never in all my life saw anything like it*.

PART II

STRESS IN WORD-FORMATION

CHAPTER 9

GENERAL

§108. So far we have been concerned chiefly with the variations in stress which occur in the inflections of Russian words. Stress also plays an important part in the derivation of words of various kinds from original roots by the addition of prefixes or suffixes or by uniting two or more distinct words in compounds. Little will be said here about compounds, but more attention will be paid to the stress of words, particularly nouns and adjectives, derived by suffixation.

§109. In compound words the stress is usually on the second (or last) element, e.g. парохо́д *steamship*, пылесо́с *vacuum-cleaner*, авторучка *fountain pen*, фотоаппара́т *camera*, книгоизда́тель *publisher*, головокруже́ние *giddiness*, колхо́з *collective farm*; второстепе́нный *secondary*, десятиле́тний *ten-year*, междунаро́дный *international*, головокружи́тельный *vertiginous*; руководи́ть *to direct*, злоупотребля́ть *to abuse*.

In some compounds the first element may have secondary stress, e.g. кнѝгоизда́тель *publisher*, гра̀мза́пись *recording* (cf. §7).

There are some exceptions with stress on the first element, e.g. ру́копись *manuscript*, жи́вопись *painting*, во̀доросль *seaweed*.

§110. Stress on a prepositional prefix is fairly common in nouns derived from verbs, e.g. по́черк *handwriting*, о́трасль *branch*, при́стань *quay*, до̀вод *reason*; and in parts of certain verbs (cf. §§93, 94); but is rare in adjectives except those derived from such verbs, e.g. и́збранный *selected*.

For the prefix вы- see §§11, 68, 93*b*.

Note the variety of accentuation in nouns derived from говори́ть: го́вор *talk*, *dialect*, догово́р *treaty*, пригово́р *verdict*, разгово́р *conversation*, but за́говор *plot*, вы́говор *pronunciation*, *reproof*, and погово́рка *saying*, *proverb*.

§111. Stress in compounds tends to be fixed. Cf. §§16*d*(iii) (nouns), 41 (adjectives), 85*b* (some verbs).

§112. (*a*) The position of the accent in a noun derived from a verb, an adjective derived from a noun, or a new noun derived from an original noun, etc., may depend either on the suffix used or on the stress-type of the original word itself.

(*b*) Many of the suffixes used in deriving nouns, adjectives and verbs are either always unstressed or always stressed, irrespective of the stress of the original word. The most common of these suffixes have already been listed (see §§10, 29, 70, 73, etc.). With a suffix which is always unstressed the derivative normally retains the stress of the original word, e.g. вѐжливый *polite* — вѐжливость *courtesy*.

(*c*) The position with the suffixes which may be stressed or unstressed is more complex, depending on a variety of factors: the length of the stem of the original word (monosyllabic or two or more syllables); the position of the accent in the original word (on the stem or on the ending); whether the original word has fixed or mobile stress. Thus with several suffixes there is a general tendency for suffix and/or endings to be stressed in words derived from monosyllabic stems, or stems with stress on the endings and/or mobile stress (e.g. боль — больнóй — больнѝца *hospital*; странá — странѝца *page*; стол (столá) — столѝца *capital*), and for the suffix and endings to be unstressed in words derived from stems of two or more syllables, especially those with fixed stress (e.g. рáзный — рáзница *difference*; рабóта — безрабóтица *unemployment*). Cf. §§115*a*, 118*c*, 119, 122, 129*b*, 130*a*, 131*c*, 132*a*, 132*b*, 137*c*, 139-144.

(*d*) Frequently there is a contrast between derivatives with the same root and the same suffix, depending on whether there is a prefix or not. Even if the suffix or ending is stressed in the unprefixed derivative, the accent may nevertheless move back on to the stem in a compound with a prefix added, e.g. рывóк *jerk* — отрѝвок *fragment, excerpt*; дворéц *palace* — однодвóрец *peasant-smallholder*. Cf. §§ 113*b*, 114*k*, 115*b*, 146, 147.

(*e*) Unfortunately the actual stock of nouns or adjectives with a given suffix in modern Russian as a rule illustrates these tendencies with only relative consistency, and there are few rules entirely without exceptions. On the other hand, the position of stress in derivatives is by no means haphazard, and in the following paragraphs 'rules' for the position of stress with the most common word-forming suffixes are given in as categorical a form as possible. The basic division of suffixes into 'productive' and 'non-productive' has been ignored here, since the aim is to give guidance on the stress of types of existing words most commonly met with in speech, and not on the formation of new words.

CHAPTER 10

NOUNS

NOUN SUFFIXES: MASCULINE

The suffixes dealt with here are **-ок, -ик** (and its variants), **-ец, -тель** (and its derivatives), **-тор, -изм** and **-ист**. For others see §10.

§113. **-ок** (*a*) Nouns are derived by means of this suffix both from nouns and from verbs. From nouns of all genders, but predominantly masculine, are derived chiefly diminutives (cf. §128*b*), but also names of things and places (e.g. **перст** *finger* — **напёрсток** *thimble*; **село́** *village* — **посёлок** *settlement*). From verbs are derived nouns denoting the action (**гуде́ть** *to hoot* — **гудо́к** *a hoot*), and the result of the action (**ре́зать** *to cut* — **отре́зок** *a piece cut off*), or the performer of the action (**игра́ть** *to play* — **игро́к** *player*).

(*b*) The stress follows the same rules whether the basic word is a noun or a verb:

(i) Derivatives without prefixes all have the stress on the suffix and mobile stress (cf. §19*b*), irrespective of the stress of the original word (although in fact masculine nouns of one syllable or with mobile stress do preponderate), e.g. Diminutives: **час — часо́к; друг — дружо́к; го́род — городо́к; зверь — зверёк; ого́нь — огонёк; дура́к — дурачо́к; мужи́к — мужичо́к; пету́х — петушо́к; ло́коть — локото́к;** From verbs: **скака́ть — скачо́к** *a jump*; **свиста́ть — свисто́к** *a whistle*; **знать — знато́к** *a connoisseur* (gen.sg. **знатока́); сосать — сосо́к** *nipple*.

(ii) Derivatives with prefixes have stress on the stem and fixed stress (cf. §112*d*), e.g. from nouns: **суд — рассу́док** *reason, sense*; **ряд — поря́док** *order*; **еди́н** *one* (Slav.) — **поеди́нок** *duel*; **ла́вка** *bench, shop* — **прила́вок** *counter*; **голова́** — **заголо́вок** *title, headline*; **борода́** — **подборо́док** *chin*; **тень** — **отте́нок** *shade, nuance*; **село́** — **просёлок** *country road*; from verbs: **поступи́ть — посту́пок** *an action*; **оста́ться — оста́ток** *remainder*; **пить — напи́ток** *drink, beverage*; **взять (вз-ять) — взя́ток** *bribe*; **снима́ть — сни́мок** *photograph*; **подари́ть — пода́рок** *gift*.

The two types of stress often occur in derivatives from the same root, with or without prefix, e.g. **го́лос — голосо́к** (dimin.) — **отголо́сок** *echo*; **расти́ — росто́к** *a sprout, shoot* — **подро́сток** *a youth*.

просёлочная дорога

Отрочество

(*c*) Several apparent exceptions are words in which -ок is not a suffix, but part of the stem, e.g. потоло́к *ceiling*, о́трок *lad*, со́рок *forty*, ры́нок *market*, ту́рок *Turk*, за́мок *castle* (cf. §4).

Exceptions with -ок as a suffix include руба́нок *plane*; рису́нок *drawing*; боти́нок *boot*; пре́док *ancestor*; пото́мок *descendant*; желу́док *stomach*; деся́ток *ten*.

(*d*) The suffix -ёнок/-онок, denoting the young of animals, is always stressed on the ё, e.g. кот — котёнок *kitten*; медве́дь — медвежо́нок *bear cub*. Cf. §10*a*.

§114. -ик (*a*) The basic suffix -ик occurs chiefly in diminutives from masculine nouns (cf. §128*a*), but it is also used to derive from adjectives a few nouns denoting persons and things (see below). In its extended forms -овик/-евик, -ник, -овник, -чик, -щик it is used to form a variety of types of noun, such as:

Diminutives, e.g. шкаф — шка́фчик; па́лец — па́льчик;
Performers of an action, e.g. носи́ть — носи́льщик; клевета́ть
    to slander — клеветни́к;
Occupations, e.g. мя́со — мясно́й — мясни́к *butcher*; лета́ть —
    лётчик *airman*;
Things, e.g. день — дневни́к *diary*;
Places, e.g. руда́ *ore* — рудни́к *mine*.

рудни́к у minierals
рудни́к у rain

cf also рудни́к - a pris (surtn)

(*b*) As a diminutive suffix -ик is always unstressed, e.g. нос — но́сик; дом — до́мик; except for мужи́к *peasant* (cf. §128*a*). In other functions -ик is always stressed and the noun has mobile stress (cf. §19*b*), e.g. ста́рый — стари́к *old man*; тупо́й *blunt* — тупи́к *cul-de-sac*; матери́к *continent*.

(*c*) In words with the extended suffix -овик/-евик stress is with very few exceptions on the last syllable (and therefore mobile, cf. §19*b*), e.g. груз *cargo* — грузово́й — грузови́к *lorry*; передово́й *leading* — передови́к *foremost worker*; большеви́к *Bolshevik*.

(*d*) -ник. Of the total number of nouns with this suffix the great majority have the suffix unstressed, usually retaining the stress of the original word and having fixed stress, e.g. па́мять *memory* — па́мятник *monument*; колхо́з — колхо́зник *collective farmer*; железнодоро́жник *railwayman*; проти́вник *opponent*; пра́здник *festival*. But a considerable number of common words, especially those derived from masculine and feminine nouns of one or two syllables, have stress on the suffix (and therefore mobile, cf. §19*b*), e.g. день — дневни́к *diary*; лес — лесни́к *woodman*; проводни́к *conductor* (*on a train*); учени́к *pupil*; воротни́к *collar*.

A few pairs of nouns with this suffix are differentiated by the stress, e.g. лéдник *ice-box* and леднúк *glacier*.

(*e*) With the extended suffix -овник stress is usually on the second last syllable, and fixed, e.g. сад — садóвник *gardener*; любóвь — любóвник *lover*; чин — чинóвник *official*.

(*f*) In nouns of all types with the suffix -чик stress is always on the second last syllable and fixed, e.g. извóзчик *old-style cabbie*; дивáнчик *divan* (dimin.); перевóдчик *interpreter*.

(*g*) -щик. The position is as with -ник (see (*d*) above) — of the total number of nouns with this suffix, the great majority, including many nouns of specialised occupations, have stress on the stem, but the ten percent with stress on the suffix include many frequently used nouns. Examples include: unstressed — барабáнщик *drummer*; тюрéмщик *gaoler*; кáменщик *stone-mason*; фрезерóвщик *milling-machine operator*; красúльщик *dyer*; stressed — танцевщúк *dancer*; часовщúк *watchmaker*; ямщúк *coachman* (archaic); временщúк *palace favourite*.

(*h*) In diminutives formed from nouns with stress on the suffix -ик, the stress moves on to the diminutive suffix -ок/-ек and is mobile (cf. §19*b*), e.g. старúк — старичóк; воротнúк — воротничóк; whereas in those with stress on the stem it is fixed in the diminutive also, e.g. рабóтник — рабóтничек. Cf. §3.

(*j*) Feminine nouns derived from nouns with all forms of the suffix -ик retain the stress of the masculine noun. The most common suffix is -ица, -ница, e.g. колхóзник — колхóзница; ученúк — ученúца; любóвник — любóвница; перевóдчик — перевóдчица; таджúк — таджúчка.

(*k*) The tendency to variation in stress between prefixed and unprefixed derivatives is seen in some nouns in -ик (cf. §112*d*), e.g. свечнúк *candlemaker*, but подсвéчник *candlestick*.

§115. -ец (*a*) With this suffix the tendency is for stress to be on the suffix and therefore mobile (cf. §19*b*) with monosyllabic stems, but on the stem and fixed with stems of two or more syllables, e.g. отéц *father*, конéц *end*, купéц *merchant*, певéц *singer*, рубéц *scar*, вдовéц *widower*; but иностáнец *foreigner*, красноармéец *Red Army man*, ленингрáдец *Leningrader*.

Most polysyllabic words in -ец have the stress on the second-last syllable, but frequently if the stem from which the word is derived has an earlier stress it is retained (especially with suffix -овец/-евец), стáлинец *Stalinist*, бéженец *refugee* (from бéгать), стахáнов_ец

Stakhanovite, по́ловец *Polovtsian*, ву́зовец *student* (from вуз *higher educational institution*). Cf. §112*c*.

Exceptions to the general rule include some monosyllabic stems with unstressed suffix, e.g. бра́тец *brother* (dimin.), не́мец *a German*, го́рец *a highlander*, ста́рец *old man, elder*, па́лец *finger*, пе́рец *pepper*, ра́нец *satchel* (German *Ranzen*), та́нец *dance* (German *Tanz*); and a few polysyllabic stems with stress on the suffix, e.g. молоде́ц *fine fellow*, продаве́ц *salesman*, жеребе́ц *stallion*, образе́ц *pattern, model*.

(*b*) With another element prefixed, stress may shift back on to the stem (cf. §112*d*), e.g. творе́ц *creator* — чудотво́рец *wonder-worker*; продаве́ц *salesman* — книгопрода́вец *bookseller*; боре́ц *fighter, champion* — иконобо́рец *iconoclast*.

(*c*) Names of the citizens of a country or town, ending in **-ец**, have the accent on the stem, usually on the same syllable as in the original place-name. Those ending in **-а́нец, -и́нец, -е́ец, -йец**, however, are as a rule stressed on the second-last syllable, whatever the stress of the original place-name, e.g. Ленингра́д — ленингра́дец *Leningrader*; Кита́й — кита́ец *a Chinese*; Шотла́ндия — шотла́ндец *a Scotsman*; Ура́л — ура́лец *a person from the Urals*; Баку́ — баки́нец *citizen of Baku*; Украи́на — украи́нец *Ukrainian*; but Ита́лия — италья́нец *Italian*; А́фрика — африка́нец *African*; Аме́рика — америка́нец *American*; Я́лта — ялти́нец *citizen of Yalta*; Евро́па — европе́ец *European*; Бе́льгия — бельги́ец *Belgian*; И́ндия — инди́ец *Indian* (of India), инде́ец *Red Indian*.

(*d*) Feminine nouns formed from nouns ending in **-ец** in general retain the stress of the masculine, but the formation varies, e.g. не́мец — не́мка *German*; краса́вец — краса́вица *handsome man / pretty woman*; певе́ц — певи́ца *singer*; продаве́ц — продавщи́ца *salesman/woman*; иностра́нец — иностра́нка *foreigner*; комсомо́лец — комсомо́лка *member of the Y.C.L.*; ленингра́дец — ленингра́дка *Leningrader*; америка́нец — америка́нка *American*; but note кита́ец — кита́янка *Chinese*; саме́ц *male animal* — са́мка *female*.

(*e*) This suffix sometimes occurs in diminutives — see §128*c*.

NOUN SUFFIXES: FEMININE

§116. Feminine forms corresponding to masculine nouns denoting persons have a variety of suffixes, some of which have been treated above (cf. §§114*j*, 115*d*, 117*b*).

(*a*) The most common suffix for this purpose is **-ка**. Derived nouns with this suffix retain the stress of the masculine noun (**-ка** is never stressed — cf. §10*b*), e.g. студе́нт — студе́нтка *student*; москви́ч — москви́чка *a Muscovite*; сибиря́к — сибиря́чка *a Siberian*; журнали́ст — журнали́стка *journalist*; официа́нт — официа́нтка *waiter/waitress*; грузи́н — грузи́нка *a Georgian*; англича́нин — англича́нка *Englishman/woman*. Note the change of stress in граждани́н — гражда́нка *citizen*.

(*b*) The less common suffix -ша, formerly used to denote the wife of an official and now used in a way roughly corresponding to *-ess* in English, is always unstressed, the noun retaining the stress of the original masculine, e.g. бригади́рша *Brigadier's wife*; конду́кторша *conductress*; библиоте́карша *librarian*.

(*c*) For nouns with the suffix -ица corresponding to masculine nouns in -тель, -ик, -ец see §§125*b*, 114*j*, and 115*d* respectively. This suffix also occurs in e.g. цари́ца *Tsarina*; Богоро́дица *Our Lady*.

(*d*) Some **female animals** have special names (e.g. су́ка *bitch*, кобы́ла *mare*) but many are derived from the masculine names by means of the suffixes -ица and -иха. These suffixes are usually stressed, e.g. лев — льви́ца *lioness*; волк — волчи́ца or волчи́ха *she-wolf*; осёл — осли́ца or осли́ха *she-ass*; тигр — тигри́ца *tigress;* слон — слони́ха *cow-elephant*. Note, however, медве́дь — медве́дица *she-bear*.

The suffix -иха is also used to form the feminine form for some occupations, e.g. по́вар — повари́ха *cook*; портно́й *tailor* — портни́ха *tailoress*; ткач — ткачи́ха *weaver*.

(*e*) -иня. This suffix is usually stressed, e.g. боги́ня *goddess*, герои́ня *heroine*, графи́ня *countess*; but a few nouns retain the stress of the masculine, e.g. мона́хиня *nun*.

Other feminine noun-suffixes

Only -ка, -ица, -ина, -инка, -ость are dealt with here. For others see §10.

§117. (*a*) -ка is widely used to form nouns of a variety of types. It is never stressed, so that the accent falls either on the stem or on an intermediate suffix like -ов. Stress is usually on the second-last syllable irrespective of its position in the original word, and is fixed, e.g. до́ярка *milkmaid* (from дои́ть *to milk*); подгото́вка *preparation* (from подгото́вить); стро́йка *building* (from стро́ить); отвёртка *screwdriver* (from отвёртывать); откры́тка *postcard* (from откры́тое письмо́); пятиле́тка *Five-year plan* (from пятиле́тний план); командиро́вка *official mission* (from командирова́ть); путёвка *travel warrant* (from путь).

(*b*) For -ка in forming feminine nouns from masculines denoting persons, see §116; and for -ка as a diminutive suffix see §129*a*.

§118. -ица. Of the total number of nouns with this suffix, more than three quarters have the accent falling on the stem.

(*a*) In feminine nouns formed from masculines ending in **-ик, -ец, -тель,** and also in a group of nouns denoting containers for specific substances, stress is on the same syllable as in the original noun, e.g. **ученик** — **ученица** *pupil* (cf. §114*j*); **красавец** — **красавица** *handsome man/woman* (cf. §115*d*); **учитель** — **учительница** *a teacher* (cf. §125*b*); **чайница** *tea-caddy*; **чернильница** *inkpot*; **пепельница** *ashtray*.

(*b*) In diminutives with the suffix **-ица** stress varies: see §129*b*.

(*c*) In nouns denoting things and conditions, stress may be on the suffix **-ица** if the basic stem is monosyllabic, stressed on the ending, or has mobile stress, e.g. **больница** *hospital*, **столица** *capital*, **черепица** *roof-tile*, **рукавица** *mitten*. Other words with **-ица** stressed (apart from those in (*a*) and (*b*) above) include: **единица** *unit*, **теплица** *hothouse*, **петлица** *buttonhole*, **горчица** *mustard*, **таблица** *table* (*of figures*), **граница** *frontier*, **ресница** *eyelash*.

In most nouns of four or more syllables in **-ица,** stress is on the stem, e.g. **гостиница** *hotel*, **безработица** *unemployment*, **путаница** *confusion*, **нескладица** *nonsense*, **пуговица** *button*, **лиственница** *larch*, **пословица** *proverb*.

Some nouns of only three syllables ending in **-ица** have stress on the stem, e.g. **мельница** *mill*, **разница** *difference*, **умница** *clever person*, **ножницы** *scissors*. Cf. §112*c*.

§119. The suffix **-ина** has a variety of functions and possibilities for stress.

(*a*) Abstract nouns denoting qualities (derived from adjectives) almost all have stress on the final syllable **-ина** (and mobile stress if plural forms exist, cf. §22*a*), e.g. **глубина** *depth*, **ширина** *width*, **величина** *size, magnitude*, **тишина** *quietness*. But note **истина** *truth*.

(*b*) Many nouns in **-ина** derived from other nouns tend to be stressed according to the stress of the original noun (cf. §112*c*), as follows: if the basic noun has fixed stress on the stem, then the derivative in **-ина** retains the stress of the basic noun, e.g. **рыба** — **рыбина** *single* (*large*) *fish*; but if the basic noun has stress on the ending in the nom. sing., or mobile stress, then the stress falls on **-ина** e.g. **скот** (**скота**) *cattle* — **скотина** *a single beast*.

Categories conforming (relatively well) to this pattern are:

(i) Names of the meat of various animals, birds and fish, e.g. **баран** (fixed stress) *ram* — **баранина** *mutton*; **телёнок** (pl. **телята**) *calf* — **телятина** *veal*; **свинья** *pig* — **свинина** *pork*; **осётр** (осетра́) *sturgeon* — осетри́на; конь (коня́) *horse* — кони́на *horse-flesh*. An exception is ло́сось (masc.) *salmon*, with fixed stress — лососи́на.

(ii) Nouns denoting a single unit or piece, derived from collective nouns and names of substances, e.g. горо́х *peas* — горо́шина *a pea*; жемчу́г *pearls* — жемчу́жина *a pearl*; лёд (льда) *ice* — льди́на *piece of ice, ice-floe*; дробь (gen.pl. дробе́й) *shot* — дроби́на *pellet of shot*; дуб (дуба́) *oak* — дуби́на *club*.

(iii) Nouns expressing large size (augmentatives) and often distaste or contempt, e.g. уро́д (fixed stress) *monster* — уро́дина *terrible monster*; дом (pl. дома́) — доми́на *big house*.

(iv) Nouns with the suffix -щина usually retain the stress of the nouns from which they are derived, e.g. ба́рщина *peasants' obligatory labour on landlord's land*, Смоле́нщина *Smolensk province*, обло́мовщина *Oblomovism*, Пугачёвщина *the Pugachov revolt*, Столы́пинщина *Stolypin's regime*. In a few nouns (mainly having corresponding adjectives with suffix -ово́й) stress falls on -щина, e.g. годовщи́на *anniversary* (cf. годово́й); but also чертовщи́на *devilry* (adj. чёртов or черто́вский). In some shorter nouns the щ belongs not to the suffix but to the stem, e.g. морщи́на *wrinkle*, лощи́на *hollow*, толщина́ *thickness*.

There are, however, many exceptions to this tentative rule, particularly in the groups which follow:

(c) In two categories of nouns stress usually falls on the suffix -ина. They are:

(i) Nouns denoting substances and tissues and many special terms in weaving, e.g. древеси́на *xylem, woody tissue* (from де́рево); паруси́на *sail-cloth* (from па́рус). Note as an exception ржа́вчина *rust* (cf. §76).

(ii) Foreign words, e.g. рези́на *rubber*, дисципли́на *discipline*, турби́на *turbine*. But note дю́жина *dozen*.

(d) For many nouns in various categories — persons, plants, lands, things — no general rule can be given, e.g. мужчи́на *man*, же́нщина *woman*, дружи́на *prince's bodyguard*; мали́на *raspberry plant*, ряби́на *rowan tree*, сморо́дина *currant bush*, бузина́ *elderberry tree*; ро́дина *native land*, о́бщина *village commune*, окра́ина *outlying districts*, Украи́на *Ukraine*; лы́сина *bald patch*, равни́на *plain*, целина́ *virgin lands*; пружи́на *spring*, корзи́на *basket*, ра́ковина *shell* (*of crustacean*), *sink*, хи́жина *hovel*. Мир жизнью и война дворцам!

§120. -инка is a suffix with the same function as -ина in §119b(ii), i.e. the derivation of nouns denoting single parts or units from collective nouns. (Some nouns with this suffix are in fact diminutives of nouns in **-ина.**) Stress is usually on the suffix, e.g. **пыли́нка** *speck of dust,* **снежи́нка** *snowflake,* **роси́нка** *dewdrop,* also **нови́нка** *a new thing, novelty*; but in a few words the stress of the original is retained, e.g. **соло́ма** — **соло́минка** *a straw*; **виногра́д** — **виногра́динка** *a grape*; **бу́сы** (no sing.) *beads* — **бу́сина, бу́синка** *a bead.*

§121. **-ость** is used in forming abstract nouns from adjectives.

(*a*) The accent never falls on this suffix, and the stress of the original word is usually retained, e.g. **го́рдый** — **го́рдость** *pride*; **све́жий** — **све́жесть** *freshness*; **опа́сный** — **опа́сность** *danger,* **о́пытный** — **о́пытность** *experience.*

Adjectives with stressed endings form abstract nouns either with the suffix **-отá,** e.g. **слепо́й** — **слепота́** *blindness*; **глухо́й** — **глухота́** *deafness*; or with the suffix **-ость,** moving the stress back on to the stem, e.g. **сухо́й** — **су́хость** *dryness*; **живо́й** — **жи́вость** *liveliness*; **молодо́й** — **мо́лодость** *youth.* (Cf. §§10*b, g.*)

(*b*) Nouns formed from adjectives with the form of passive participles retain the stress of the participle (cf. §125*c* below), e.g. **непроница́емый** — **непроница́емость** *impenetrability*; **незави́симый** — **незави́симость** *independence*; **убеждённый** — **убеждённость** *conviction*; **пре́данный** — **пре́данность** *devotion.* Also e.g. **сто́ить** — **сто́имость** *cost, value,* **реши́ть** — **реши́мость** *resolution,* with no corresponding adjectives.

NOUN SUFFIXES: NEUTER

Only the two suffixes **-ство** and **-ние** warrant special treatment here. (See also §10.)

§122. **-ство,** which forms abstract and collective nouns, is usually unstressed, the stress of the original word being retained, e.g. **де́тство** *childhood,* **ра́бство** *slavery,* **крестья́нство** *peasantry,* **студе́нчество** *students, the student body,* **произво́дство** *production,* **строи́тельство** *construction* (cf. §125*a*(ii)), **о́бщество** *society.*

There is, however, a considerable number of nouns with stress on the suffix **-ство,** mainly derived from nouns or verbs with final or mobile stress, e.g. **Рождество́** *Christmas,* **вещество́** *substance,* **существо́** *being, creature,* **большинство́** *majority,* **мастерство́** *masterly skill,* **хвастовство́** *boasting.* Stress in these is fixed except for the gen. pl. where it exists, e.g. **веще́ств, суще́ств** (cf. §18).

§123. For stress of nouns with suffix **-ание** or **-ение,** see §125 below.

SOME FAMILIES OF DERIVATIVES

§124. A number of the most common productive suffixes used in forming nouns and adjectives (particularly from verbs) can be grouped into families having characteristic rules of stress.

§125. (*a*) The two most important formations from verbs are nouns with the suffix **-тель** denoting the performer of an action (person or thing) and those with the suffix **-ние** denoting the action itself or the product of the action.

The stress in both of these types of noun follows the same pattern, depending on the conjugation:

(i) Nouns formed from verbs with infinitive in **-ать** have suffixes **-атель** and **-ание**, and retain the stress of the infinitive, e.g.

писа́ть — писа́тель *writer* — писа́ние *writing*
слу́шать — слу́шатель *listener* — слу́шание *a hearing*
основа́ть — основа́тель *founder* — основа́ние *foundation*
иссле́довать — иссле́дователь *investigator* — иссле́до-
вание *investigation*

(ii) Those from verbs with infinitives in **-еть, -ить** and 'monosyllabic' verbs in **-сть, -зть, -чь** and **-ти**, have suffixes **-и́тель** and **-е́ние**, with stress on the suffix irrespective of the stress of the original verb, e.g.

учи́ть — учи́тель *teacher* — уче́ние *teaching, studies*
пра́вить — прави́тель *ruler* — правле́ние *government*
стро́ить — строи́тель *builder* — строе́ние *building*
спасти́ — спаси́тель *rescuer, saviour* — спасе́ние *salvation*

There are some exceptions to this rule, e.g. дви́гать — дви́га-тель *motor*, but движе́ние *movement*; обеспе́чить (pfv.) *to ensure* — обеспе́чение *guarantee*; сосредото́чить (pfv.) *to concentrate* — сосредото́чение *concentration*; ве́дение *authority*, све́дение *knowledge, information*, музыкове́дение *musicology* (all from the archaic verb ве́дети *to know*); Благове́щение *the Annunciation*; наме́рение *intention*. The noun *discovery* may be stressed either обнару́жение or обнаруже́ние. Two nouns derived from ви́деть are differentiated by stress: ви́де-ние *sight, vision (sense)*, and виде́ние *vision, apparition*. Stress in these nouns is fixed. (учи́тель is an exception: see §20*a*.)

Благове́щение

(*b*) Stress of further derivatives based on nouns with suffix **-тель**, including the feminine form in **-ница**, is the same as that of nouns in **-тель**. (In many cases a 'basic' form in **-тель** does not, in fact, exist although adjectives or nouns 'formed' from it do.) e.g.

APGRS H

учи́тель — учи́тельница	teacher
учи́тельский съезд	teachers' conference
поучи́тельная исто́рия	didactic story
поучи́тельность	instructiveness
предста́вить — представи́тель(ница)	representative
представи́тельная систе́ма	system of representation
представи́тельство	representation
представи́тельствовать	to act as a representative
представле́ние	representation

исключи́ть (pfv.) *to exclude* — исключи́тельный *exclusive, exceptional* (there is no noun исключи́тель)

(*c*) On the other hand nouns with suffix -ость derived from present and past passive participles retain the stress of the participle, e.g.

ви́деть — ви́димый — ви́димость *visibility*

образова́ть — образо́ванный — образо́ванность *'educatedness'*

изыска́ть (pfv.) *to find* — изы́сканный — изы́сканность *refinement*

Note the considerable number of adjectives in -имый and nouns derived from them, which have the form of present participles passive, but are derived from perfective verbs. In them the stress sometimes differs from that of the infinitive, e.g.

раствори́ть (pfv.) *to dissolve* — раствори́мый *soluble* — раствори́мость *solubility*

оспо́рить (pfv.) *to dispute* — неоспори́мый *indisputable.* Cf. §65.

§126. (*a*) A rather similar group of derivatives connected with verbs is that of the many relatively recent coinings (largely of 'international' terms) in the technical and political fields corresponding to such English words as *organise, organiser, organisation, organisational,* etc., e.g.

организова́ть — организа́тор — организа́ция

механизи́ровать — механиза́тор — механиза́ция

All such nouns have the stress on the suffixes -а́тор and -а́ция (but for the stress of verbs with suffix -овать see §73).

(*b*) Further derivatives from these nouns may retain this stress, e.g. adjectives in -ский: организа́торский тала́нт *ability as an organiser*; but adjectives in -онный have the accent on the adjectival suffix, e.g. организацио́нный комите́т *organisational committee* (cf. §29).

Nouns formed from passive participles have the stress of the participle, e.g. организо́ванность рабо́ты *well-organised state of work.*

§127. (*a*) A further family of related types of words is that of the
-isms and *-ists*. The suffixes **-изм** and **-ист**, as well as the frequently
associated **-ик** and **-ический**, are always stressed, and further derivatives from them have the same stress, e.g.

> социали́зм *Socialism* — социали́ст — социалисти́ческий
>   *Socialist*
> большеви́зм *Bolshevism* — большеви́к — большеви́стский
>   *Bolshevik*
> реали́зм *realism* — реали́ст — реалисти́ческий *realist*(*ic*)

Abstract nouns in **-ика**, and associated agent nouns in **-ик**, however, have unstressed suffixes, e.g.

> журнали́ст, fem. журнали́стка *journalist* — журнали́стский
>   *journalistic* — журнали́стика *journalism*
> матема́тика *mathematics* — матема́тик *mathematician* —
>   математи́ческий *mathematical*

(*b*) Derivatives from this group and those in §126 are often associated, e.g.

> специализи́ровать *to specialise* — специализа́ция *specialisation*
>   — специа́льность *speciality, profession* — специали́ст *spe-*
> *cialist* — специали́зм *narrow specialisation.*

DIMINUTIVES

The suffixes used in forming diminutives of nouns are given below
in four groups: one for each gender of basic nouns and the fourth
for suffixes used in common with nouns of more than one gender.

Masculine diminutive suffixes

§128. (*a*) **-ик**. Many masculine nouns form diminutives by means
of the suffixes **-ик** or **-чик**, which are always unstressed, the stress of
the original noun being retained, e.g. **до́мик** *little house,* **го́дик** *year,*
ро́тик *mouth,* **шка́фчик** *little cupboard,* **автомоби́льчик** *car,* **коло-
ко́льчик** *little bell* (with shift of stress from **ко́локол**). The stress
is fixed.

For **-ик** in functions other than as a diminutive suffix see §114.

(*b*) **-ок** is always stressed in diminutives (cf. §113*b*) and the accent
is mobile (cf. §19*b*). Some nouns form diminutives in both **-ок** and
-ик, with corresponding difference in stress, e.g. **год** — **годо́к**, **го́дик**
year; **рот** — **рото́к**, **ро́тик** *mouth;* **листо́к** *leaf,* **голосо́к** *voice,* **денёк**
day, **огонёк** *little light.*

A further diminutive suffix may be added to such diminutives in
-ок. The accent remains on the **-о-** of the first diminutive suffix and

is fixed in declension, e.g. цвет — цвето́к — цвето́чек *flower*; бе́рег — бережо́к, бережо́чек *bank, shore*. The plurals of these would therefore be цветки́, бережки́ but цвето́чки, бережо́чки.

(*c*) -ец. This suffix is less commonly used to make diminutives. Where it is, stress is always on the stem and fixed, e.g. брат — бра́тец (gen. sing. бра́тца) *brother*; моро́з — моро́зец *frost*.

For -ец in general see §115.

Feminine diminutive suffixes

§129. (*a*) The most common feminine diminutive suffix is -ка. The stress of diminutives with this suffix is fixed on the stem, even if the original noun has stress on the endings or mobile stress, e.g. кни́га — кни́жка *book*; берёза — берёзка *birch*; доро́га — доро́жка *road, path*; дочь — до́чка *daughter*; дыра́ — ды́рка *hole*; вода́ *water* — во́дка *vodka*; статья́ — стате́йка *article*; рука́ — ру́чка *hand, handle*; стрела́ — стре́лка *hand of a clock*. The stress is fixed. (Cf. §117*a*.)

In forming further diminutives from nouns ending in -ка the suffixes -очка/-ечка or -онька/-енька are used, the accent remaining on the same syllable as in the first diminutive, e.g. ды́рочка, кни́жечка, во́дочка, берёзонька, доро́женька, до́ченька, ру́ченька.

Some diminutives are formed directly from the basic noun by the addition of these 'double diminutive' suffixes, although the form with the first degree of diminution in -ка either does not exist or is seldom used, e.g. ма́ма — ма́мочка *mother* (ма́менька is rather old-fashioned, ма́мка means *wet-nurse*); па́па — па́почка *father* (but па́пка means *a folder, file*); душа́ — ду́шечка or ду́шенька *soul, darling* (ду́шка is *a nice person*, ironically); звезда́ — звёздочка *star*.

(*b*) -ица. Stress in diminutives with this suffix depends on that of the basic noun: if it is of the third declension (e.g. часть) or has mobile stress, the accent falls on the diminutive suffix, e.g. страна́ *country* — страни́ца *page*; вода́ — води́ца *water*; сестра́ — сестри́ца *sister*; часть *part* — части́ца *particle*; вещь — вещи́ца *thing*; if, however, the basic noun in -а has fixed stress, the accent remains on the stem in the diminutive, e.g. про́сьба — про́сьбица *request*; ро́ща — ро́щица *grove*. (An exception is деви́ца *spinster*.)

Stress in all nouns in -ица is fixed (cf. §112*c*).

Further diminutives may be formed from these by adding the suffix -ка, the stress remaining as in the first diminutive, e.g. страни́чка, сестри́чка, води́чка.

(*c*) The suffix -ца is less commonly used to form diminutives. Stress is usually on the ending: лень *laziness* — ленца́ (он с ленцо́й *he's rather lazy*); кре́пость *fortress* — крепостца́; but note дверь — две́рца *door*.

Stress is fixed on the same syllable as in the nominative singular.

(*d*) To express a certain amount of contempt the suffix -онка/ -ёнка is used. This is always stressed (contrast with -онька, -енька above §129*a*, which are always unstressed), e.g. кни́га — книжо́нка; руба́шка — рубашо́нка *shirt*; ло́шадь — лошадёнка *horse*. (Сестрёнка, however, expresses affection.)

A few masculine nouns form such contemptuous diminutives, e.g., мужи́к *peasant* — мужичо́нка.

Stress is fixed.

Neuter diminutive suffixes

§130. (*a*) The most commonly used diminutive suffixes for neuter nouns are -це, -ице when unstressed, and -цо́, -ецо́ when stressed (cf. §3). In general nouns with stress on the stem in the nom. sing. have the unstressed suffixes, and those with stress on the ending in the nom. sing. have the stressed suffixes, but there are many exceptions. Examples are: блю́до *dish* — блю́дце *saucer*; де́ло — де́льце *affair*; зе́ркало — зе́ркальце *mirror*; пла́тье — пла́тьице *dress*; вино́ — винцо́ *wine*; письмо́ — письмецо́ *letter*; ружьё — ружьецо́ *gun*. (Cf. §112*c*.)

Exceptions include: сло́во — словцо́ *word*; о́зеро — озерцо́ *lake*; пи́во — пивцо́ *beer*; стекло́ *glass* — стеко́льце *pane*; окно́ — око́нце *window*; полотно́ *linen* — полоте́нце *towel*. For the word де́рево *tree* both forms occur: де́ревце or деревцо́.

The stress in the plural is normally fixed on the same syllable as in the nom. sing. of the diminutive irrespective of the stress of the original noun, e.g. де́льце — де́льца, словцо́ — словца́. But озерцо́ is exceptional, with pl. озёрца. (Cf. §20*b*.)

(*b*) A few neuter nouns form diminutives with the suffix -ко, most of them having stress on the stem even if the original noun has stress on the endings, e.g. о́блако — о́блачко *cloud*; я́блоко — я́блочко *apple*; лицо́ — ли́чико *face*; колесо́ — колёсико *wheel*; окно́ — око́шко *window*. The following, however, have stress on the endings: молоко́ — молочко́ *milk*; о́ко *eye* — очко́ *point, mark*, очки́ *spectacles*.

(*c*) 'Double' diminutives may be formed from both of the above types of diminutive by adding a further suffix -ко. The stress is always on the stem or first diminutive suffix even if the first diminutive has stress on the endings, e.g. слóво — словцó — словéчко; блю́до — блю́дце — блю́дечко; окнó — окóшко — окóшечко; крылó *wing* — крыльцó *porch* — крылéчко.

Some neuter nouns have first diminutives with this form, e.g. сéрдце — сердéчко *heart*; мéсто — местéчко *place*.

(*d*) Note that the nom. pl. of nouns with suffix -ко has the vowel и and fixed stress, e.g. я́блочки, колёсики, окóшки, словéчки. Óблачко is exceptional in retaining both the ending and the stress of the plural of óблако, i.e. облачкá.

Common diminutive suffixes

Some diminutive suffixes are used for all genders, the vowel endings in themselves not being indicative of the gender, which remains that of the original noun whatever the diminutive ending.

§131. -ушка, -ушко as a diminutive suffix is always unstressed, the accent falling on the syllable before the suffix, whatever the stress of the basic word, e.g. дед — дéдушка *grandfather*; дя́дя — дя́дюшка *uncle*; гóлубь — голýбушка *pigeon*; бáтюшка *father* (from colloquial бáтя); женá — жёнушка *wife*; мать — мáтушка *mother* (archaic and familiar); дéва *maid* — дéвушка *girl*; головá — голóвушка *head*; пóле — пóлюшко *field*; мóре — мóрюшко *sea*.

Exceptions include избá *peasants' house* — избýшка; кóмната *room* — комнатýшка.

This suffix occurs under stress in many nouns which are no longer felt to be diminutives, e.g. верхýшка *summit*, веснýшка *freckle*, кукýшка *cuckoo*; and also in diminutives of nouns with the suffix -ухá, e.g. старýха — старýшка *old woman*.

See §133c and *d* for -ушка in diminutives of Christian names.

(*b*) The diminutive and usually rather contemptuous suffix -ашка always bears the accent, whatever the stress of the basic noun, e.g. старúк — старикáшка *old man*; мúлая — милáшка *pretty woman*.

(*c*) Nouns of all genders form diminutives usually with a shade of contempt or irony with the suffix -ишка, -ишко. (Masc. nouns have -ишка if they denote animate beings, -ишко for inanimates.) The position of the accent depends on the stress of the basic word (cf. §112c): if it has mobile stress the accent in the diminutive falls on the suffix, e.g. вор — ворúшка *thief*; гóрод — городúшко *town*; дом — домúшко *house*; земля́ — землúшка *land*; письмó — письмúшко *letter*; ружьё — ружьúшко *gun*. If the stress of the original noun is fixed then it is on the stem in the diminutive, e.g. офицéр — офицéришка *officer*; забóр — забóришко *fence*; погóда — погóдишка *weather*; плáтье — плáтьишко *dress*.

There are some exceptions, e.g. мáльчик — мальчúшка *boy*.

The nom. pl. of nouns in both -ка and -ко end in и (cf. §130*d*).

Further diminutives are sometimes formed from these by the addition of the suffix -ка or -ко, e.g. мальчи́шечка.

(*d*) The suffix -ышко is used, mainly with neuter nouns but also occasionally with masculines (-ышек), to form diminutives with no contemptuous overtones. It is always unstressed, the accent falling on the stem and being fixed even if the basic noun has stressed endings, e.g. воробе́й *sparrow* — воро́бышек; со́лнце — со́лнышко *sun*; гнездо́ — гнёздышко *nest*.

(*e*) Diminutives in paragraphs (*c*) and (*d*) above ending in -ко have the nom. pl. ending in и, e.g. городи́шки, пла́тьышки, гнёздышки. Cf. §130*d*.

Augmentative suffixes

§132. Augmentatives, denoting large size and very often contempt or irony, are formed with the suffixes -ище, -ища and -ина.

(*a*) With -ище/-ища the position of the accent is dictated by the stress of the basic noun (cf. §112*c*): if it has fixed stress the accent in the augmentative usually remains on the stem, e.g. арбу́з *water-melon* — арбу́зище; челове́к — челове́чище *enormous fellow*; кни́га — кни́жища *huge tome*; but if the stress of the basic noun is mobile, the accent falls on the suffix -ище, -ища, e.g. доми́ще *huge house*; друг — дружи́ще *friend*; окни́ще *window*; нож — ножи́ще *knife*; нога́ — ножи́ще *leg, foot*.

Augmentatives of masculine nouns in -ище have the nom. pl. in и, e.g. ножи́щи *knives*.

Stress in these augmentatives is fixed.

(*b*) Stress in augmentatives with the suffix -ина conforms to the same rule, e.g. ры́ба — ры́бина *large fish*; доми́на *big house*; лоб — лби́на *forehead*.

For -ина in other functions see §119.

Chapter 11

PROPER NAMES

Diminutives of Christian names

The possibilities of forming diminutives from Russian Christian names are almost unlimited, but in stress they conform to clear-cut rules.

§133. The first diminutive, on which most further diminutives are based, is always stressed on the syllable before the ending, i.e. usually the first syllable, since most are disyllabic, e.g.

Алекса́ндр — Са́ша	Мари́я, Ма́рья — Ма́ша
Алексе́й — Алёша	Михаи́л — Ми́ша
Бори́с — Бо́ря	Ната́лья — Ната́ша
Валенти́на — Ва́ля	Никола́й — Ко́ля
Варва́ра — Ва́ря	О́льга — О́ля
Вита́лий — Ви́тя	Па́вел — Па́ня, Па́ша
Влади́мир — Воло́дя	Пётр — Пе́тя
Гали́на — Га́ля	Серафи́ма — Си́ма
Дми́трий — Ми́тя	Степа́н — Стёпа
Екатери́на — Ка́тя	Татья́на — Та́ня
Елизаве́та — Ли́за	Со́фья — Со́ня
Ива́н — Ва́ня	Ю́рий — Ю́ра
Любо́вь — Лю́ба	Я́ков — Я́ша

(b) Diminutives with the following suffixes always retain the stress of this first diminutive:

-ка   e.g. Ва́нька, Ка́тька, Пе́тька, Са́шка, etc.

-ечка   e.g. Ва́нечка, Ми́шечка, Со́нечка, Та́нечка, etc.

-енька e.g. Бо́ренька, Ка́тенька, Ми́тенька, Ната́шенька, Са́шенька, etc., also Ли́занька

-ик   e.g. Ми́тик, also Па́вел — Па́влик

(c) Diminutives with the following suffixes always have stress on the suffix:

-уша   e.g. Ваню́ша, Катю́ша, Павлю́ша, Петру́ша, Таню́ша, etc.

-ушка   e.g. Ваню́шка, Катю́шка, etc. An exception is Со́нюшка.

-ок~ёк e.g. Филиппо́к, Ванёк, Танёк

(d) Diminutives in **-ушка** formed not from the first diminutive but directly from the full name, however, retain the stress of the full name,

e.g. Екатери́нушка, Степа́нушка, Ива́нушка, etc. Петру́шка
from Пётр is an exception which is to be expected since Пётр has
mobile stress.

Patronymics

§134. (*a*) Most patronymics are formed from the father's Christian
name by means of the suffixes **-ович, -евич** (masc.) and **-овна, -евна**
(fem.). The stress of the father's Christian name is retained, and the
suffix is almost invariably unstressed, e.g. Ива́н — Ива́нович, Ива́-
новна; Па́вел — Па́влович, Па́вловна; Влади́мир — Влади́ми-
рович, Влади́мировна; Васи́лий — Васи́льевич, Васи́льевна.
In the patronymics from Михаи́л stress shifts on to the **a** and the
и is shortened to **й**: Миха́йлович, Миха́йловна.

The patronymic suffix is stressed only in Петро́вич, Петро́вна.
(Пётр is unusual in having mobile stress — on the endings throughout, cf. §19*a*.)

Note the contrast in stress between the suffix **-ович** here in patronymics (unstressed) and in surnames (stressed) — see §135*d*.

The unstressed syllables in patronymics tend to disappear in speech,
and the pronunciation of the suffixes **-ович** and **-овна** as they are
written is almost never heard: Ива́нович is regularly pronounced as
if written Ива́ныч, and Ива́новна as Ива́нна, while a long name
like Алекса́ндрович is reduced in normal speech to something like
Алекса́ныч or even [ˈsanitʃ]. Similarly

Миха́йлович [mɪˈxalitʃ]	Миха́йловна [mɪˈxalnə]
Алексе́евич [aɭɪˈkṣeɪtʃ]	Алексе́евна [aɭɪˈkṣevnə]
Влади́мирович [vlaˈdim̩ritʃ]	Влади́мировна [vlaˈdim̩ɪrnə]

Stress in these patronymics is fixed.

(*b*) The few male Christian names ending in **-a** form patronymics
with the suffixes **-ич** (masc.) and **-ична, -йничка** (fem.), e.g. Ники́та
— Ники́тич, Ники́тична; Илья́ *Elias* — Ильи́ч, Ильи́нична;
Фома́ *Thomas*—Фоми́ч, Фоми́нична; Кузьма́—Кузьми́ч, Кузь-
ми́нична. If the Christian name has stress on the ending, the masc.
patronymic in **-ич** always has stress on the suffix in the nom. sing.
and moving on to the endings in all other cases (cf. §19*b*), e.g. **речь
Влади́мира Ильича́ Ле́нина** *a speech by Lenin*.

Surnames

§135. Russian surnames having the same suffix may have the stress
on different syllables, e.g. Гера́симов, Кирса́нов, Пирого́в or
Му́соргский, Даниле́вский, Шаховско́й. The same name indeed
may be stressed in different ways by different people, e.g. Ива́нов

or **Иванóв, Никúтенко** or **Никитéнко**; the position of stress being dictated by family tradition or personal taste.

For the overwhelming majority of surnames, however, there exists a normal form, and for each common surname suffix there is a normal accentuation as described below.

(*a*) **-ов, -ев.** Surnames with this suffix show most variation in stress—it may be on the suffix, the penultimate syllable or an earlier syllable. About sixty percent of surnames in **-ов, -ев**, however, have stress on the penultimate syllable, e.g. **Грибоéдов, Давы́дов, Чéхов, Зинóвьев, Карамáзов, Катáев, Менделéев, Крю́ков, Мáйков, Набóков, Обломов, Пáвлов, Потáпов, Семёнов.**

Stress on the last syllable is next in order of frequency, and many of these names are derived from masculine nouns with mobile stress (monosyllabic nouns and those with such stressed suffixes as **-ак, -ок, -ук, -ун, -ар**, etc.—cf. §19*b*) or other nouns with stress on the ending in the nom. sing. Examples are: **Попóв, Ежóв, Петрóв, Бобрóв, Козлóв, Соловьёв, Хрущёв, Чулкóв, Каткóв, Лескóв, Кирпичóв, Хомякóв, Каблукóв, Казакóв, Хлестакóв, Кузнецóв, Лихачёв, Пугачёв, Годунóв, Глазунóв, Комарóв, Гончарóв, Крылóв, Кольцóв.**

The majority of surnames with such derivation conform to this rule, but there are a few exceptions, e.g. **Язы́ков, Аксáков, Булгáков, Вóлков, Сумарóков.**

Surnames of three or more syllables with accent on the antepenultimate or earlier syllable include many derived from nouns with the suffix **-ик, -ник**, and also from other nouns with stress fixed on an earlier syllable, e.g. **Мéльников, Хлéбников, Корабéльников, Нóвиков, Чúриков, Бáтюшков, Лéбедев, Мóлотов, Сáхаров, Яковлев, Фёдоров, Кáменев, Лéрмонтов, Сúмонов, Чúчиков.**

Feminine forms of these surnames preserve the stress of the masculine, e.g. **Пáвлова, Бáтюшкова, Крылóва, Кузнецóва.**

Stress is fixed, e.g. **мýзыка Глазунóва** *Glazunov's music*.

Note that the general rule for writing **е** or **о** after **ж, ч, ш, щ** and **ц** (cf. §3) does not always hold for surnames, so that e.g. **Грибачев, Хрущев** are pronounced with the suffix **-ев/-ов** stressed: **Грибачёв, Хрущёв.**

(*b*) **-ин.** Nearly all surnames ending in **-ин** have the accent on the penultimate syllable irrespective of the form of the stem, e.g. **Бакýнин, Боборы́кин, Бухáрин, Держáвин, Есéнин, Калúнин, Карéнин, Лéнин, Прúшвин, Пýшкин, Стáлин, Столы́пин, Голúцын,** etc.

Very few have stress on an earlier syllable, e.g. **Кýрочкин.**

A small proportion have stress on the suffix, including e.g. **Бороди́н, Головы́н, Ильи́н, Карамзи́н, Княжни́н, Купри́н, Кузьми́н, Луки́н, Щедри́н**, etc. (several of these are derived from Christian names or other nouns with stress on the endings: **Илья́, Лука́, Кузьма́, борода́, голова́**).

Surnames in **-ин** (like those in **-ов**) are in origin possessive adjectives and decline with mixed endings, e.g. **стихи́ Пу́шкина, о Пу́шкине, с Пу́шкиным; Анна Каре́нина, Анну Каре́нину, к Анне Каре́ниной, об Анне Каре́ниной**.

Those with stress on the suffix in the nom. sing. masc. have mobile stress, shifting on to the endings in all forms, including the feminine, e.g. **я ви́дел господи́на Ильина́** *I saw Mr. Ilyin*; **переда́йте приве́т Ильину́** *Give my regards to Ilyin*; **я был с господи́ном Ильины́м** *I was with Mr. Ilyin*; etc. **э́то госпожа́ Ильина́** *This is Mrs. Ilyin*; **я говори́л с госпожо́й Ильино́й** *I was speaking to Mrs. Ilyin*; etc. **я был у Ильины́х** *I was at the Ilyins'*. Cf. patronymics §134*b*.

(*c*) **-ский**. A very high proportion of surnames ending in **-ский** have stress on the penultimate syllable, whatever the form of the stem, e.g. **Бараты́нский, Бели́нский, Маяко́вский, Ми́рский, Оболе́нский, Остро́вский, Спера́нский, Чайко́вский, Черныше́вский**.

Note the frequent contrast in stress between surnames derived from the same root with suffixes **-ов** and **-овский**, e.g. **Жу́ков — Жуко́вский; Алекса́ндров — Александро́вский; Андре́ев — Андре́евский; Ива́нов — Ивано́вский; Миха́йлов — Михайло́вский; О́сипов — Осипо́вский; Па́влов — Павло́вский**.

Note also the contrast between the same name in **-ский** used as a surname and as a place name. In the latter the stress is normally on the same syllable as in the basic noun (usually a Christian name), e.g. **село́ Алекса́ндровское; Ива́новский райо́н; село́ Миха́йловское; Па́вловский райо́н**.

The much smaller number of surnames in **-ский** with stress on an earlier syllable include: **А́нненский, Вя́земский, Ке́ренский, Ли́говский, Му́соргский, Одо́евский**. *Литово*

Only a very small number of surnames have the stressed ending **-ской**, e.g. **Крамско́й, Трубецко́й, Шаховско́й**.

Surnames in **-ский** decline as adjectives and in all forms, including the feminine, retain the stress of the nom. sing. masculine, e.g. **Ми́рская, Михайло́вская, Трубецка́я**.

(*d*) **-ович, -евич**. Surnames with this suffix all have stress on the penultimate syllable, e.g. **Григоро́вич, Максимо́вич, Серафимо́вич, Шостако́вич, Казаке́вич, Паске́вич, Станке́вич**.

They often show a contrast in stress with surnames from the same root with suffix -ов, e.g. Анто́нов — Антоно́вич; Богда́нов — Богдано́вич; Андре́ев — Андре́е́вич (cf. §135c).

Note the contrast in stress between surnames in -ович and patronymics with this suffix (cf. §134a), e.g. Михайло́вич (surname) — Миха́йлович (patronymic).

Surnames in -ович decline as nouns in the masculine only. Stress is fixed. There is no feminine form, the form of the nom. sing. masculine being used for all cases in the feminine, e.g. А́нна Петро́вна Антоно́вич; я говори́л с А́нной Петро́вной Антоно́вич.

(e) -ич. In general surnames with this suffix (including those above with -ович), have the accent on the penultimate syllable, e.g. Ву́лич, Гне́дич, Мику́лич. *Зачёты*

Masculine surnames in -ич decline with fixed stress, but there is no feminine form and they are indeclinable for women, e.g. я говори́л с Татья́ной Гне́дич.

(f) -енко. About half of the surnames with this suffix are stressed on the penultimate syllable and half on an earlier syllable, e.g. Короле́нко, Косте́нко, Шевче́нко, but Авсе́енко, Да́нченко, Зо́щенко.

As a rule they do not decline either for men or women, e.g. расска́з Короле́нко *a story by Korolenko*.

(g) -ак and -ук. These suffixes are usually stressed, e.g. Пастерна́к, Пильня́к, Корнейчу́к.

They have no feminine forms, and are indeclinable for women. For men they decline as nouns with stress on the endings, e.g. про́за Пильняка́ *Pilnyak's prose* (cf. §19b), except Пастерна́к which has fixed stress.

(h) The stress of Russian surnames with other forms is unpredictable, but they are relatively few, e.g. Толсто́й (cf. the adj. то́лстый), Полево́й, Наре́жный, Жива́го (indeclinable), Сологу́б, Кантеми́р, etc.

(j) Surnames of non-Russian peoples of the Soviet Union include many with characteristically stressed suffixes (apart from those which have been given a Russian form and conform therefore to the rules above, e.g. Абдулла́ев). The most common of these are:

(i) Georgian. Stress is on the penultimate syllable with suffixes -дзе, -ели, -или, -ани, e.g. Чавчава́дзе, Орджоники́дзе, Кецхове́ли, Джугашви́ли, Орбелиа́ни. These are indeclinable in Russian.

(ii) Many Armenian names end in the suffix -ян which is always stressed, e.g. Хачатуря́н, Сарья́н, Микоя́н. These, like most non-Russian surnames ending in a consonant, decline as nouns for men, but are indeclinable in the case of women.

CHAPTER 12

ADJECTIVES

§136. Adjectives may be stressed on the stem (кла́ссовый), on a derivative suffix (столо́вый), or on the endings (мирово́й).

The most common suffixes which are either always stressed or always unstressed have been listed in §§29, 125b, 126b, 127a. Here we shall deal with suffixes having some or all of the above possibilities for stress.

§137. In adjectives with the following suffixes the accent may fall either on the stem or the suffix:

(a) **-овный/-евный.** Stress is almost invariably on the penultimate syllable, e.g. духо́вный *spiritual*, душе́вный *of the soul, mental*, церко́вный *ecclesiastical*, верхо́вный *supreme*.

(b) **-ичный.** The stress depends on that of the word from which the adjective is derived, as follows:

(i) In all adjectives derived from nouns (with almost exclusively foreign or 'international' roots) ending in -ика, -ия, or otherwise corresponding to English adjectives ending in *-ic(al)*, stress is on the penultimate syllable, irrespective of the stress of the basic word, e.g. фа́брика — фабри́чный *factory*; ло́гика — логи́чный *logical*; мело́дия — мелоди́чный *melodious*; анало́гия — аналоги́чный *analogous*; типи́чный *typical*; перви́чный *primary*. Many of these have 'doublets' with the suffix -ический, e.g. фантасти́чный — фантасти́ческий; академи́чный — академи́ческий.

(ii) In adjectives derived from Russian nouns (ending chiefly in -ица, but some in -ик, -ич, etc.) stress is as in the basic noun, e.g. у́лица — у́личный *street*; пра́здник — пра́здничный *festive*; столи́ца — столи́чный *capital*; больни́ца — больни́чный *hospital*; кирпи́ч — кирпи́чный *brick*.

(c) With the two suffixes **-истый** and **-ливый** the general tendency is for stress to be on the suffix in adjectives derived from monosyllabic stems or those with stressed endings or mobile stress, but on the stem with polysyllabic stems or those with fixed stress (cf. §112c), e.g. холм — холми́стый *hilly*; тень — тени́стый *shady*; сон — сонли́вый *sleepy*; дождь — дождли́вый *rainy*; серебро́ — серебри́стый *silvery*; скала́ — скали́стый *rocky*; гора́ — гори́стый *mountainous*; слеза́ — слезли́вый *tearful*; хло́поты — хлопотли́вый *trouble-*

some, fussy; but глина — глинистый *of clay*; болото — болотистый *marshy*; морщина — морщинистый *wrinkled*; талант — талантливый *talented*; совесть — совестливый *conscientious*; жалость — жалостливый *compassionate*.

The examples above are all derived from nouns. With adjectives derived from verbal roots the situation is slightly different: with the suffix -истый stress is always on the stem, e.g. отрывать — отрывистый *jerky*; раскатиться—раскатистый *rolling*. With -ливый, the stress is on the suffix with monosyllabic roots, either on the stem or the suffix with disyllabic roots, and always on the stem with roots of three or more syllables, retaining the stress of the original verb, e.g. monosyllabic stems: крикливый *clamorous*; хвастливый *boastful*; молчаливый *taciturn*; disyllabic stems: терпеливый *patient*; говорливый *talkative*; понятливый *quick to understand*; догадливый *perspicacious*; услужливый *obliging*; longer stems: надоедливый *boring, tiresome*; словоохотливый *garrulous*.

Exceptions derived from nouns with fixed stress, but having stress on the suffix include: шумливый *boisterous*; счастливый *happy*; мясистый *fleshy*; золотистый *golden*.

§138. The position with types of derived adjective which may be stressed on the endings is more complicated. Those with suffixes -ов-, -овск-, -енн- and -ан- have three possibilities for stress—on stem, suffix or ending, e.g. дедовский *grandfather's*, отцовский *paternal*, воровской *thievish*; while with -н- and -ск- added directly to the stem there are only two possibilities, e.g. женский *female*, мужской *male*, местный *local*, больной *ill*.

No account is taken here of non-derivative 'basic' adjectives (e.g. слепой, дурной, голубой) which have been dealt with in §§36-44 above.

Adjectives derived from nouns are dealt with in §§139-146, and those with verbal stems and stressed endings in §147.

§139. With the suffixes specified in §138 the general tendency mentioned in §112c again applies: polysyllabic stems and those with fixed stress tend to have the accent on the stem of the adjective, while those with monosyllabic stems and mobile stress tend to stress either the suffix or the endings. Thus about half of the monosyllabic and disyllabic nouns with mobile stress listed in §§19-25 form adjectives with stressed endings. The most common of these are:

With suffix -ной: §19: дневной *of a day*; §20: лесной *forest*, родной *native, dear*, цветной *coloured*, поездной *of a train*; §21: грудной *breast, suckling*, очередной *next in turn, recurrent*, степной *steppe*, **цепно́й** *chain*, **дверно́й** *door*, **областно́й** *regional*, **крепост-но́й** *of a fort*, *serf-*, **ночно́й** *nocturnal*, **площадно́й** *of a square*, **зуб-но́й** *dental*, **коренно́й** *radical*; §23: **спинно́й** *back*, **земно́й** *terrestrial*; §24: **свечно́й** *of a candle*, **строчно́й** *of a line*, *small* (*letter*); §25: **головно́й** *head*, **ножно́й** *of the leg*, **речно́й** *river*, **ручно́й** *hand*, *manual*, **стенно́й** *wall*, *mural*.

With suffix **-яно́й**: §19: **льняно́й** (from **лён**) *linen*; §21: **шерстя-но́й** *woollen*; §22: **избяно́й** *of a peasant's house*, **травяно́й** *of grass*, **водяно́й** *water*, *aquatic*.

With suffix **-ово́й**: §19: **ножево́й** *of a knife*, **трудово́й** *labour*, **ледово́й** *of ice*, **полково́й** *regimental*; §20: **боево́й** *of battle*, **боко-во́й** *side*, **верхово́й** *mounted*, **годово́й** *year's*, **дымово́й** *smoke*, **мехово́й** *fur*, **мирово́й** *world*, **мостово́й** *bridge*, *roadway*, **носово́й** *nose*, **часово́й** *hour*, as noun: *sentry*, **городово́й** *pre-*1917 *policeman*, **берегово́й** *of the shore*, **полево́й** *field*, **делово́й** *business*(*-like*), **поло-во́й** *floor*, *sexual*, **фронтово́й** *front-line*; §22: **гнездово́й** *of a nest*, **зернаво́й** *cereal*, **кольцево́й** *ring*. Cf. also **сороково́й** *fortieth*.

With suffix **-ско́й**: §20: **мужско́й** *male*, **городско́й** *municipal*, **мастерско́й** *craftsman's*, as fem. noun: *workshop*, **морско́й** *nautical*.

With suffix **-овско́й**: §21: **воровско́й** *thievish*.

§140. Many of the nouns in these lists, however, form adjectives with stress on the suffix, e.g.

§19: **дворо́вый** *of a yard*, **днепро́вский** *of the Dnieper*, **столо́вый** *table*, *dining-room*, **кремлёвский** *Kremlin*, **рублёвый** *of a rouble*, **льви́ный** *lion's*, **ледови́тый** *Arctic*, **врачє́бный** *medical*, **королє́в-ский** *royal*. This includes some of the masculine nouns with stressed suffixes and mobile stress, e.g. **старико́вский** *old man's*, **дворцо́вый** *palace-*, **образцо́вый** *model*, **отцо́вский** *paternal*. (See also §144 below.)

§20: **садо́вый** *garden*.

§21: **лошади́ный** *of a horse*, **церко́вный** *ecclesiastical*, **волоса́-тый** *hairy*, **черто́вский** *devilish*, **лебеди́ный** *swan's*.

§22: **винова́тый**, **вино́вный** *guilty*, **вое́нный** *military*, **скали́-стый** *rocky*, **сосно́вый** *pine*, **стекля́нный** *of glass*.

§23: **душе́вный** *of the soul*, *mental*.

§24: **волни́стый** *wavy*.

§141. A considerable number of the nouns in §§19-25, however, although having mobile stress form adjectives with stress on the stem, e.g.

§19: **вра́жеский** *enemy*, *hostile*, **у́мный** *intelligent*, **ца́рский** *Tsar's*, *royal*, **со́нный** *sleepy*, **вре́дный** *harmful*, **сты́дный** *shameful*.

§20: дру́жный, дру́жеский *friendly*, кня́жеский *princely*, ра́йский *of Paradise*, хле́бный *of bread*, щёлковый *silken*, вече́рний *evening*, холо́дный *cold*, ле́тний *summer*, ме́стный *local*, небе́сный *heavenly*, серде́чный *hearty, sincere*, слове́сный *verbal*, о́блачный *cloud*.

§21: ка́менный *stone*, вла́стный *imperious*, сме́ртный *mortal*, ча́стный *private*.

§22: бе́дный *poor*, весе́нний *spring*, гла́вный *principal*, же́нский *female*, звёздный *starry*, ну́жный *necessary*, сре́дний *middle*, суде́бный *legal, of a court*, лу́нный *lunar*, ви́нный *of wine*, пи́сьменный *written*, руже́йный *of a gun*, се́льский *village*, я́дерный *nuclear*.

§23: во́дный *water-*, зи́мний *wintry*, це́нный *valuable*.

§24: слёзный *of tears*, де́нежный *of money*, похоро́нный *funeral*.

§25: го́рный *mountainous, mining*.

§142. Adjectives derived from monosyllabic nouns having fixed stress usually keep the accent on the stem (but cf. §143), e.g. ба́нковый, ба́нковский *banking-*, га́зовый *gas-*, джа́зовый *jazz*, кла́ссовый *class-*, ма́ссовый *mass-*, пла́новый *planned, systematic*, ро́зовый *pink*, а́вгустовский *August*, ву́зовский *of a higher educational institution*, де́довский *grandfather's*, ко́жаный *of leather*.

But some have stress on the suffix, e.g. фрукто́вый *fruit*, граммо́вый *of a gram*, почто́вый *postal*.

§143. A considerable number of short nouns with fixed stress do, however, form adjectives with stressed endings, e.g. грузово́й *cargo-*, фунтово́й *one-pound*, бытово́й *of everyday life*, звуково́й *sound-*, страхово́й *insurance*, духово́й *wind* (*instrument*), запасно́й *reserve, spare*, цехово́й *workshop*, группово́й *group-*, основно́й *basic*, больно́й *ill*, обувно́й *footwear-*, кровяно́й *of blood*, мясно́й *of meat*, пивно́й *of beer*.

These may, of course, form other adjectives with stress on the stem or suffix, e.g. зву́чный *sonorous*, стра́шный *terrible*, духо́вный *spiritual*, etc.

§144. Most adjectives formed from nouns of two or more syllables retain the stress of the original noun, even if it has mobile stress, e.g.

from nouns with fixed stress: фарфо́ровый *porcelain*, апельси́новый *orange*, кероси́новый *paraffin*, поря́дковый (from поря́док) *serial*, etc.

from nouns with mobile stress (mainly lists in §§19 and 20): мужи́цкий *peasant's*, коне́чный *terminal*, купе́ческий *merchant's*, учени́ческий *of a pupil*, дура́цкий *foolish*, каза́цкий *Cossack*, кирпи́чный *brick*, бага́жный *luggage-*, сапо́жный *boot-*, таба́чный *tobacco*, -эта́жный *-storied*, профе́ссорский *professorial*. Some of these shift

the stress, e.g. ко́локол — колоко́льный *of bells*, дере́вня — дере-
ве́нский *village*, де́рево — деревя́нный *wooden*.

For adjectives derived from some masculine nouns with stressed
suffixes cf. §140.

§145. Adjectives with suffix -енный formed from longer nouns and
nouns with fixed stress usually retain the stress of the original noun,
e.g. жизнь — жи́зненный *of life, vital*; боле́знь — боле́зненный
morbid; фо́рма—бесфо́рменный *formless*; соло́ма—соло́менный
straw; мгнове́ние — мгнове́нный *instantaneous*; обыкнове́ние —
обыкнове́нный *habitual, ordinary*; ка́чество — ка́чественный
quality; госуда́рство — госуда́рственный *state*. Note the shift of
accent in those derived from nouns ending in -ство with final stress,
e.g. вещество́ — веще́ственный *substantial*; существо́ — суще́ст-
венный *essential*; торжество́ — торже́ственный *solemn*; and also
о́бщество — обще́ственный *social*.

Adjectives in -енный from neuter nouns in -мя vary: пла́мя —
пла́менный *ardent*; but и́мя — именно́й *nominal* (and adv. и́менно
specifically). Вре́мя has both вре́менный *temporary* and временно́й
to do with time, temporal, e.g. вре́менное прави́тельство *the Pro-
visional government*; временна́я систе́ма *system of tenses*.

§146. Note the difference in stress in some compound adjectives with
prefixes, e.g. веково́й *of centuries*—средневеко́вый *medieval*; днев-
но́й *of a day* — ежедне́вный *daily* (cf. §112*d*).

§147. An additional group of **adjectives with stressed endings** is de-
rived by means of the suffix -н- from verbal roots, chiefly with prefixes,
e.g. выходно́й *exit*. The total number of such verbal roots is small,
including such groups as ходи́ть, води́ть and other verbs of motion,
класть, ста́вить and similar verbs, some of the monosyllabic verbs
in -ить (e.g. бить), etc. Here again the tendency to shift the accent
back on to the stem in compounds is evident (cf. §112*d*): although
with prepositional prefixes the stress is on the endings, it normally
shifts on to the stem when the prefixed element is a noun or adjective,
e.g. записно́й, прописно́й etc., but живопи́сный *picturesque*, руко-
пи́сный *hand-written*.

(*a*) With the following stems all adjectives with suffix -н- (except
those compounded with nouns) have stress on the endings:

-бив- (бить) e.g. набивно́й *printed* (*calico*)

-шив- (шить) e.g. вышивно́й *embroidered*

-плав- (пла́вать) e.g. сплавно́й *floatable*

-дув- (дуть) e.g. надувно́й *inflatable, pneumatic*

-иск- (иска́ть) e.g. сыскно́й *investigational*
-кид- (кида́ть) e.g. откидно́й *folding, collapsible*
-пис- (писа́ть) e.g. записно́й *for notes*; прописна́я бу́ква *capital letter*
-пуск- (пуска́ть) e.g. отпускно́й *holiday*
-сып- (сы́пать) e.g. рассыпно́й *sold loose, by weight*

(*b*) With the following stems nearly all derived adjectives have stress on the endings (except compounds and some formed from well-established nouns like уе́зд *district*):

-движ- (дви́гать) e.g. подвижно́й *mobile*, задвижно́й *sliding*; but подви́жный *agile*
-езд- (е́здить) e.g. поездно́й *of a train*, проездна́я пла́та *fare*, etc.; but уе́здный *district*
-зыв- (звать) e.g. призывно́й *recruiting*; but призы́вный *inviting*
-клад- (класть) e.g. прикладно́й *applied* (*art*), складно́й *folding, collapsible*; but скла́дный *well-ordered, well-made*
-куп- (купи́ть) e.g. покупно́й *purchased*, etc.; but подку́пный *open to bribes*
-лив- (лить) e.g. проливно́й *torrential*, заливно́й луг *water-meadow*, заливна́я осетри́на *jellied sturgeon*
-рез- (ре́зать) e.g. резно́й, вырезно́й *carved*, etc.; but хлебо-ре́зный нож *breadknife*
-став- (ста́вить) e.g. составно́й *component, composite*, подстав-но́й *dummy*, etc.
-сталь- (стать) e.g. остально́й *remaining*, etc.; but при́сталь-ный *fixed, intent*
-тяж- (тяну́ть) e.g. втяжно́й *suction-*, etc.; but протя́жный *drawn-out, slow*

(*c*) With the following stems about half of the adjectives with suffix -н- have stress on the endings, and half on the stem:

-вод- (води́ть) e.g. заводно́й *clockwork*, etc.; but вво́дный *introductory*, перево́дный *translated*
-каз- (-каза́ть) e.g. заказно́й *made to order*; *registered* (*letter*); показно́й *showy, ostentatious*
-рыв- (рыть and рвать) e.g. подрывно́й *undermining, subversive*, взрывно́й, разрывно́й *explosive*; but e.g. непреры́вный *continuous*
-ход- (ходи́ть) e.g. входно́й *entrance*, выходно́й *exit*, проход-но́й *communicating* (*door*); but перехо́дный *transitional, transitive*, схо́дный *similar*, etc.
-воз- (вози́ть) e.g. вывозно́й *export*, привозно́й or приво́зный *imported* but вво́зный *import*

(*d*) Among other verbal roots occurring in adjectives with stressed endings are **-вар- (варить)**, **-вес- (висеть)**, **-лож- (-ложить)**, **-мыв- (мыть)**, **-нос- (носить)**, **-плыв- (плыть)**, **-сев- (сеять)**, **-ступ- (ступать)**.

§148. Possessive adjectives are derived from nouns by means of the suffixes **-ов/-ев** and **-ин**. The former is no longer productive and appears now only in fixed phrases.

(*a*) Most possessive adjectives in **-ов** retain the stress of the original noun, e.g. **Иванов день** *St. John's day*, **Юрьев день** *St. George's day*, **Пифагорова теорема** *Pythagoras' theorem*, **Баренцево море** *Barents sea*, **крокодиловы слёзы** *crocodile tears*, **чёртова дюжина** *baker's dozen*. Those derived from nouns with mobile stress have stress on the suffix, e.g. **отцовы слова** *one's father's words*, **рождество Христово** *Christ's nativity*. Stress is fixed in both types.

(*b*) Possessive adjectives in **-ин** retain the stress of the original noun, e.g. **дядин** *uncle's*, **сукин** *of a bitch*, **бабушкин** *grandmother's*, **материн** *mother's*, **братнин** *brother's*, **Троицын день** *Trinity Sunday*; and from diminutives: **мамин** *Mummy's*, **папин** *Daddy's*, **Машин** *Masha's*, **Володин** *Volodya's*.

Those derived from nouns with stress on the endings may shift the accent on to the stem, e.g. **сестра — сестрин** *sister's*, **жена — женин** *wife's*, or in the case of some Christian names stress the suffix: **Фома — Фомин** *Tom's*. In the latter case the endings are stressed in all other forms, e.g. **Фомина книга** *Tom's book*, **из Фоминой книги** *out of Tom's book*, etc. (Cf. surnames in **-ин** §135*b*).

SELECT BIBLIOGRAPHY

Avanesov, R. I. and Ozhegov, S. I. Русское литературное произношение и ударение: словарь-справочник. Moscow, 1959. Lists only words in which there could be any doubt (for Russians) about pronunciation or stress: words not included may be presumed to have fixed stress.

Bylinskii, K. I. Словарь ударений для работников радио и телевидения. Moscow, 1960. Intended for radio announcers: more narrowly prescriptive than the above, aiming to give only one 'normal' form for any word. Haphazard in selection, but contains many personal and geographical names.

Ozhegov, S. I. Словарь русского языка. Moscow, 1960. The most recent one-volume dictionary of Russian. Like the bigger dictionaries gives very full information on the stress of each word, including a positive indication of fixed stress.

Vinogradov, V. V. and others. Грамматика русского языка. Moscow, Академия Наук СССР, 1952-54. Vol. 1, Morphology, deals with stress, but despite the authoritative source and fulness of treatment the lists of examples show some inaccuracies.

Unbegaun, B. O. *Russian Grammar*. Oxford, 1957. Gives a general treatment of stress for each part of speech.

Avanesov, R. I. Ударение в современном русском литературном языке. Moscow, 1958. A general discussion of the principles of Russian stress.

Matthews, W. K. *Russian Historical Grammar*. London, 1960. Pp. 178-187 give a brief historical review of Russian stress.

Kiparsky, V. Der Wortakzent der russischen Schriftsprache. Heidelberg, 1962. A detailed study of the stress patterns of all parts of speech, taking into account the present-day norms and all available evidence of earlier patterns in Russian and in other Slavonic and Baltic languages.

Ward, Dennis. *Russian Pronunciation: A Practical Course*. Edinburgh, 1958. A clear, up-to-date account with reference to recent Russian sources.

Boyanus, S. C. *Russian Pronunciation*. London, 1955.

For further titles on both practical and theoretical aspects see:

Unbegaun, B. O. *A Bibliographical Guide to the Russian Language*. Oxford, 1953. Items 209-220, 660-677.

REFERENCE INDEX

All references are to sections, not pages.

All words quoted in Part I, and those in Part II which are derived from words in Part I, are listed here. In addition a considerable number of words with fixed stress which may be considered part of the essential vocabulary have been included.

Many common nouns with fixed stress and suffixes **-ия**, **-ость**, **-ство** and **-ние** have, on the other hand, been excluded: they are covered categorically by the rule in §16c.

All nouns, adjectives and verbs have been marked F (fixed) or M (mobile). In the latter case the reference immediately following is to the section(s) in which the basic stress pattern is described, and further references are to other relevant sections. References following a semi-colon are to Part II and therefore as a rule to words derived from the entry-word. F in brackets (F) means stress fixed except for some isolated case, e.g. masc. locative in **-у́**.

With verbs (M) indicates that while the basic verb has fixed stress – having no past participle passive – compounds have this participle stressed in accordance with the pattern concerned.

All suffixes mentioned have been listed.

To avoid constant reference to the body of the book the most frequently recurring stress patterns are recapitulated here in minimum form with their section references:

19   стол, стола́   *pl.* столы́, столо́в
20   мост, мо́ста   *pl.* мосты́, мосто́в
     сло́во, сло́ва   *pl.* слова́, слов, слова́м
21   год, го́да   *pl.* го́ды, годо́в
22   страна́, страну́   *pl.* стра́ны, стран, стра́нам
     окно́, окна́   *pl.* о́кна, о́кон, о́кнам
23   душа́, ду́шу, души́   *pl.* ду́ши, душ, ду́шам
24   губа́, губу́   *pl.* гу́бы, губ, губа́м
25   рука́, ру́ку, руки́   *pl.* ру́ки, рук, рука́м
37   прав, права́, пра́во, пра́вы
38   ви́ден, видна́, ви́дно, ви́дны *or* видны́
39   стар, стара́, ста́ро *or* старо́, ста́ры *or* стары́
40   хоро́ш, хороша́, хорошо́, хоро́ши
71*a*   чита́ть — чита́ет — чи́танный
72*b*   писа́ть — пишу́, пи́шет — пи́санный
73*b*   образова́ть — образу́ет — образо́ванный
80   верну́ть — вернёт — завёрнутый
85*a*   говори́ть — говори́т — говорённый/говорена́, о́, ы́
85*b*   купи́ть — куплю́, ку́пит — ку́пленный
95*a*   брать — берёт — брал, брала́, бра́ло, бра́ли — со́бранный
98*a*   нести́ — несёт — нёс, несла́, о́, и́ — принесённый/-ена́, о́, ы́